THE GENIUS OF HAIKU

Readings from R.H.Blyth
on poetry, life, and Zen

THE GENIUS OF HAIKU

Readings from R.H.Blyth
on poetry, life, and Zen

With an introduction by
James Kirkup

Published by
THE BRITISH HAIKU SOCIETY
1994

to mark the Tercentenary of the death of Matsuo Bashô
(in November, 1694), and the Thirtieth Anniversary of the
death of Reginald Horace Blyth (d. 28 October, 1964).

ACKNOWLEDGMENTS:

The British Haiku Society expresses its sincerest thanks to: Hokuseido Press, for permission to use copyright material; James W. Hackett, for access to letters he received from R.H.Blyth and Harold G. Henderson; the Museum of Haiku Literature, Tokyo, for information; Yasukoshi Kawashima, who put at our disposal his privately-printed volume of reminiscences of R.H. Blyth by former friends and students, *Kaisô no Blyth / In Memory of Blyth*, from which much biographical information was drawn; Ikuyo Yoshimura, for allowing us to refer to her as yet unpublished research into the life of R.H.Blyth in Japan, a rich source of further biographical detail; Nana Margaret Takeda, for the photograph of her father; the Wordsworth Trust, Grasmere; Joan Giroux, for appraising the manuscript; and among its own members to the following who collaborated in bringing the anthology to fruition: James Kirkup, for the Introduction and other contributions; David Cobb, who initiated the project, and served as compiler and editor; Stephen Henry Gill, for assistance with compilation and editing; Colin Blundell, Richard Goring, Jackie Hardy, George Marsh, and Brian Tasker, for advice; Penny Price for the cover calligraphy.

The Society also records its indebtedness to the Sasakawa Foundation for the financial assistance which has made publication possible.

British Library Cataloguing-in-Publication Data
A catalogue record for this book is available from the British Library.
ISBN 0 9522397 0 1

Designed and set by Ray Owen
Printed and bound by Antony Rowe Ltd., Chippenham

CONTENTS

what is more important
is to be fond of cats. Now, you see,
I have contradicted what I
wrote on the previous page, but
{who cares?
{who shares?   Yours,

FOREWORD

R. H. Blyth is better known abroad than he is in Britain, the land of his birth. His name does not appear, so far, in our *Dictionary of National Biography*, nor in the various *Who's Whos* of writers.

One of the reasons for this may be that his books have been brought out, until now, almost exclusively by two or three Japanese publishers. Another may be that his works traverse several neighbouring fields of study, and he was actually at pains to blur the distinctions between them: philosophy, religion, Eastern literature, world literature and comparative literature, English literature. He may therefore fall between lists of recommended reading in different fields.

Blyth's importance as a writer on Eastern philosophy and religions and on Eastern literatures has probably been celebrated more widely in this country, than his ability to reevaluate English literature, and especially English poetry, from the standpoint of someone familiar with the different literary traditions of the East.

The present anthology is an attempt to present Blyth to a wider public in Britain and Europe, and in the process to refocus attention, to some extent, on his very special view of poetry and life.

There is no better time to do this than in 1994, the tercentenary year of the death of Matsuo Bashô, and the thirtieth anniversary of the death of Blyth himself. Also, when we stand on the very doorstep of a new millenium may be a good time to re-present someone who held that 'we are poets in so far as we live at all'.

It may interest the reader to know what 'selection' entailed. Blyth's main works of literary criticism and philosophy run to some 6,000 pages in print (that leaves aside many hundreds of pages of student text). Even allowing for the fact that there is a good deal of repetition in the topics he discussed, the reduction to a mere 150 pages may be thought a perilous amputation. We trust the heart of Blyth's work has survived this operation.

In an effort to make the best use of space, and also in the interest of consistency, we have taken a few liberties with previously published texts. We have systematised the punctuation and use of diacriticals, where they varied from book to book. We have gone some way towards checking references to sources, and corrected a few misattributions.

1

Blyth's numerous quotations from Wordsworth's *Prelude* must have been based on a pre-World War II edition of the 1850 text, but it is not apparent which one this was. The circumstances of his internment during the War may even have meant he had to rely to some extent on memory. We have therefore revised the quotations and book/line references in accordance with the currently most authoritative edition, that published in the *Norton Critical Series*, 1979.

Editorial cuts and elucidatory additions are signalled by square brackets [ ]. A very few minor footnotes have disappeared, without brackets to indicate they have gone. Maybe some readers will be sorry to discover the omission of citations in Japanese and Chinese scripts, which Blyth almost always gave. The reason for this, apart from the need to publish at an affordable price, is that we do not expect most of our readers can read them. Blyth's transliterations, which we have kept, give an impression of the sound of the poems in Japanese, and this is generally all that is needed to follow his arguments.

INTRODUCTION

BLYTH'S WAY

Part 1: The Man

R. H. Blyth was a man so modest and self-effacing, it would never have occurred to him to write an autobiography. Our knowledge about his life is rather scanty. Almost the only reference to his life story is in the Preface to one of his books. Characteristically, this account, of only about half a page, gives no dates: it is as if his life's philosophy had led him to regard his existence on earth as beyond time.

He speaks of his 'inner destiny' predisposing him to 'pass through certain phases, which however were not mutually exclusive'. These phases included 'an inborn animism'; a natural passage to vegetarianism (strictly speaking, he was a lacto-vegetarian); the discovery of the Way of Haiku; and 'the biggest bit of luck of all, Zen, through the books of Daisetz Suzuki'. The final phase was the Way of Senryu, 'an understanding of all things by laughing or smiling at them, and this means forgiving all things, ourselves and God included'. This constituted what he called his autobiography.

Blyth was an Essex man. He was born at 93, Trumpington Road, Leytonstone, in a house overlooking two cemeteries, one Christian, the other Jewish, on 3 December, 1898, the only child of Horace Blyth and his wife, Henrietta Blyth (née Williams). (Horace was the son of a house painter, and Henrietta the daughter of an ironmonger and builder.)But before real memories began, Blyth had moved to Ilford, to live in a house in Pyrmont Road, and to attend, first, Cleveland Road Primary School, and later the County High School for Boys. His father worked as a clerk for the Great Eastern Railway. The family was poor, and Blyth would tell how he used to run along station platforms selling chocolate to train passengers; something which gave him an enduring passion for chocolate. But he was a gifted youth, with a passion for the music of Bach, and a love of literature and languages. He was strong and well-built, with a frank, open face, dark eyes, and thick, unruly brown hair.

One of the first significant events of his life occurred in 1916, during the First World War, when at the age of 18 he became eligible for conscription. He declared himself a pacifist and a conscientious objector to war, and was imprisoned in Wormwood Scrubs. Perhaps he had read Shaw's *Common Sense about the War* (1914) and the anti-war writings of Bertrand Russell. Such rejection of war required much greater courage in those jingoistic times than it would today, and the small band of pacifists were regarded as traitors to their country and outcasts from decent society. It is likely someone sent him a 'white feather', and his parents must have suffered unkind neighbourly gossip. Possibly Blyth was also influenced by the example of Max Plowman, a serving officer who declared his pacifist stand in 1916, and was court-martialled for resigning his commission. Plowman was a great influence upon me, too, and though the first time I met Blyth in Tokyo (1963) I did not know he had been a C.O., he already knew from my autobiographies published in the 1950s that I had been a war-resister, and I feel this, as well as the fact that we were both 'only children', contributed to the strong feelings of sympathy passing between us when we met in the offices of the magazine, *Orient/West*. Blyth was already in the early stages of his final illness, though he still looked hale and hearty. He spoke quietly and, unlike the cold, condescending and cagey Blunden who accompanied him, smiled at me and sent out waves of understanding.

Other influences on Blyth in his youth must have been the Tuesday and Thursday readings at the 'Poetry Bookshop' in Devonshire Street which Harold Monro had opened in 1912. Ivor Gurney, Siegfried Sassoon and Wilfred Owen were disillusioned war poets he could have met there. Perhaps he knew the work of Ralph Hodgson, who was to teach in Sendai, Japan, from 1924 to 1938. Those were stirring times in the poetry world. H.D., who was a Quaker, lived in London from 1911. Pound settled there for a while as co-editor of *Blast* from 1914-15; he had published *Personae* and *Exaltations* in 1909. He was the London editor of the *Chicago Little Review* from 1917 to 1919, and was translating much Japanese and Chinese poetry in his own inimitable way, helped along by Laurence Binyon's British Museum monographs on Chinese and Japanese prints and paintings, and by his *Japanese Art* published in 1909. Ralph Hodgson's first books, *Eve* and *Poems*, were published in 1913 and 1917, and Blyth, as a vegetarian, must have approved of his polemic against the destruction of animals to provide smart clothes for women, in the poem *To Deck a Woman.*

Blyth was already trying his own hand at poetry and translations, and two of his poems were to appear in *The London Mercury* in August, 1927.

When the war came to an end, Blyth entered London University, where he read widely in English literature and the history of language. He also studied Latin, French and Logic and graduated in October, 1923, with First Class Honours in English. In his spare time he had also taught himself enough Italian, Spanish, German and Russian to be able to read Dante, Cervantes, Meister Eckhart, Goethe (and later Hermann Hesse), as well as Dostoevsky, in the originals. What is more, he taught himself music, learning to play the organ and the flute. After graduation, he spent one year training for the teaching profession, and obtained his certificate from the London Day Training College in 1924. One of his fellow students at university was Annie Bercovitch. They fell in love, and married just before he took up his first teaching post.

It was no ordinary school in Britain where he went to teach. A Japanese scholar, Akio Fujii, had come to study at London University, with an instruction from his superiors to find some good person to teach at Keijo, which was what Seoul was called in those days when the whole of Korea was under Japanese domination. Fujii met Blyth and asked him to accept his proposal. Blyth did so straight away, without hesitation. He had already become interested in the East, chiefly India, though he was disgusted by the way British colonials treated the indigenous population. In 1924 he left England with his wife to take up a post as assistant professor at Keijo University.

It was in Korea that Blyth became seriously interested in Japanese culture, and Zen Buddhism in particular. He was deeply affected by Daisetz Suzuki's *Essays in Zen Buddhism (First Series)*, which he read in book form in 1927. He set about learning Japanese and Chinese: under Japanese occupation, Korean was a forbidden language. It is very likely that he had become acquainted with various aspects of Japanese culture even before leaving London, through the translations of Arthur Waley, and perhaps some of the writings of Yeats who was beginning to take a rather superficial interest in Zen. Blyth was to remain in Seoul teaching English language and literature for sixteen years.

Though he was only an assistant professor, he received a high salary, much more than his Japanese colleagues. Soon he was able to buy land and built a Japanese-style house and garden which filled him with delight. In Sendai, Ralph Hodgson became famous because he filled his house with birds and bred bulldogs. In Seoul, Blyth was able to express his deep love of animals by keeping dogs, goats and even horses on his land.

Among the floods of Russian and Polish refugees to Asia in the 1920s, there were many in Seoul. Among them, Blyth was often mistaken for a Russian, because though he was well paid, he dressed very simply and never smartly. Certainly his robust stature and broad face have a rather Slav aspect, reminiscent of Pasternak. His favourite form of recreation in Seoul was watching Japanese movies, then entering their first great period. They helped him acquire contemporary expressions, and also entertained him with their visual beauty and the charm of often absurd situations and dialogues.

In his *Zen and Zen Classics, Volume 1,* Blyth makes the rather mysterious assertion that a disappointment in love had driven him to Zen. Certainly there were marital difficulties, and Blyth's wife Annie parted from him and returned to England in April, 1934. But before that happened, Blyth, childless, had adopted a Korean boy of poor family, but of brilliant intelligence. Blyth took one year of absence from the university in 1935 to return home to Annie and this boy. After the divorce was ratified, Blyth returned to Korea in early 1936, leaving the adopted son with Annie. But tragedy was to ensue.

The boy was eventually to enter London University where he graduated with high honours, and after World War II he returned to Korea and became a university professor. In 1947, during the Korean War, he was captured by North Korean soldiers. Because he spoke fluent English, against his will he was made to broadcast propaganda to the UN forces. At the end of the war he was denounced to the South Korean authorities as a collaborator and shot. This was something that deeply saddened the final decade of Blyth's life. Zen Buddhism was his consolation.

But there was another, more tangible source of comfort. In 1937 he met a young Japanese woman, Tomiko, who was working in a department store in Seoul. He proposed to her, and they were married the same year. Tomiko was beautiful, and brought him great happiness in the form of children — two girls, Harumi and Nana, both lovely and intelligent, one born just before, and the other two years after the war.

During his last two years in Korea, Blyth learned to read *kanji* (the Chinese characters used in writing Japanese) quite well. His vegetarianism caused problems sometimes in a land where meat is a staple food, and is preferred to fish. During academic celebrations at the Chosun Hotel or the Keijo Hotel in Seoul, Blyth could eat only certain kinds of *sushi* like *inarizushi* and *norimaki*, while his colleagues gorged themselves on fatty *sukiyaki* and steaks. (Blyth's favourite restaurant, the 'Sushi Hisa', was in Honmachi Street, the centre of the Japanese enclave in Seoul. The owner was a great friend.) Blyth never tired of reproving the Japanese for their bad habits, for their worship of Western goods and ways. He praised the traditional Japanese greeting, a bow, so much better than kissing and shaking hands, which he said were filthy, animalistic, barbaric and unhygienic. He loved the simple things in his house and garden, even though at times he found them difficult to live with — *tatami, shôji, hibachi, o-furo,* and so on. He said, 'Truly artistic things are always impractical, inconvenient and un-utilitarian — that is what makes them beautiful.' In a sense, he was more Japanese than most Japanese. But it was his 'inner destiny' that was making him so.

When World War II broke out in 1939, Blyth left Korea for Japan with his wife and daughter and settled in Kanazawa, on the Japan Sea coast. He became a teacher of English at the Fourth High School (later to become Kanazawa University) in Kanazawa, the birthplace of his mentor and spiritual guide, Daisetz Suzuki.

But when Japan entered the war, he was interned as an enemy alien, and for the next four years lived in comparatively easy conditions (heating was a winter problem) in a house called Mark's House near the Tor Road in Kobe. His wife and daughter took up residence nearby, and he was allowed to see them once a week, giving him access to his great library, until in an air raid his wife's house, and all their possessions, were destroyed. Blyth was left with only the books he had been allowed to take into captivity. Despite this, during his internment he continued his scholarly work. *Zen in English Literature and Oriental Classics,* his first major work, was published by Hokuseido in 1942 — a brave venture, indeed, to publish in English the work of an enemy alien in time of war.

At the outbreak of war, Blyth wanted to take Japanese nationality, and he had influential sponsors: Daisetz Suzuki, Nôsei Abe (later president of Gakushûin University/ The Peers' School, in Tokyo), and Katsunoshin Yamanashi, the then President of Gakushûin, who was an old friend. But his application was turned down. Interned with him in Kobe was an American, Robert Aitken, brought over from Guam, who had been *rôshi* or master of the Hawaiian Zen *dôjô*. He and Blyth were able to practise Zen meditation together during their confinement, and Blyth also had the solace of playing his beloved silver flute. Blyth was eventually to receive compensation for his losses of property from the Japanese Government.

With the arrival of the American occupation forces, Blyth was freed and was able to play a significant part in the peace process, to the benefit of Japan. He used to say, 'If the Japanese had not given up their traditional ways, and had taken more interest in the composition of haiku and senryu, this stupid war would never have happened.' A little simplistic, perhaps, but one understands what he meant. So, after the war, he and Harold G. Henderson were prominent go-betweens in the cause of peace between Japan and the Allies.

Henderson, also a haiku scholar, was on the staff of General MacArthur's GHQ. Blyth went to see him, and learnt that MacArthur wanted to close down the Peers' School (Gakushûin University). Blyth persuaded him to let it continue, opening it to the general public. Nôsei Abe declared the university owed Blyth an immeasurable debt.

Blyth began teaching at Gakushûin after the war. He had distinguished foreign colleagues in the French scholar and haiku poet, Noël Nouet, and the German professor of philosophy, Robert Schinzinger. At the same time, Blyth became private tutor to the Crown Prince Akihito, and was to say that the Prince was the pupil he taught longest: indeed, he taught him even after his marriage to Princess Michiko, and to the end of his (Blyth's) life.

Blyth had his first meeting with the Emperor Hirohito on February 14, 1946. Their informal conversation lasted for one hour, and the Empress too was present. Through Katsunoshin Yamanashi he was able to present to the Emperor (employing the official court channels involving the Grand Chamberlain, Sukemasa Irie) a copy of *The British Royal Family in Wartime*. This popular publication was a photographic record of the activities of King George VI and Queen Elizabeth, when they visited bomb sites and air raid victims and shelters in the London Underground. In this way, Blyth was instrumental, always through intermediaries at court, in persuading the Emperor, who until the war's end had been reverenced as a deity, to undertake a journey all over Japan (excepting Okinawa) to show himself to his distressed subjects as an 'ordinary mortal'.

Blyth also had a part with Harold Henderson in drafting the Emperor's epoch-making radio speech in which he declared himself to be 'a human being', not a god. Henderson took their draft of this speech to General MacArthur, who pronounced himself very satisfied with it, and arranged for it to be translated in a style suited to the Emperor's usual mode of address.

According to Katsunoshin Yamanashi, MacArthur discussed with Blyth the question of making the Emperor change his Shinto religion. But Blyth answered that a man's religion is a sensitive personal matter, and its impulse must come from within. Therefore the Emperor should not be approached on this matter. However, Blyth said he would try to explain Christianity to members of the Imperial Family and to encourage their understanding of the Christian point of view. This led to his suggestion that the Crown Prince would benefit from being taught by a women tutor, preferably an American Quaker, and that is how Elizabeth Gray Vining came to be appointed.

On Blyth's first visit to the palace, Her Imperial Majesty, kindly trying to set him at ease, remarked that he looked very fat — Blyth loved chocolate and rich cakes. He, who in his student days had been a well-built sportsman, admitted his physical decline, saying that even elephants, who only eat leaves, also grow fat. The Empress was amused by this humorous self-deprecation.

Trained in English methods, Blyth encountered problems teaching Japanese students. In Korea, he expected them to accept and attain British standards. But these were too severe, for Japanese students prefer their university teachers to be 'kind' and not too rigorously intellectual. Eventually they went on strike, remaining dead silent when he asked them questions. However, one student stood up for his teacher: he was Kyôshi Kasai, and when they met again ten years later, Blyth remembered his courageous gesture, saying: 'It's the teacher's fault if communication with the students fails. At that time, I was very young, and accustomed to British methods and standards. I lacked humility.' Yet this was the man who arranged with the university to pay, out of his own pocket, for the education of many poor but hardworking and intelligent Korean and Japanese students.

One of Blyth's former students, the haiku scholar and translator Professor Kazuo Satô of Waseda University, tells me Blyth was an unusual teacher, who did not just read passages from his own books year in and year out, calling it 'lecturing', as did many Japanese professors. Blyth would just walk into the lecture room with a piece of chalk and begin to speak, quoting poems from memory and writing them on the blackboard for students to memorize. He never prepared a class, or never seemed to; he would simply extemporize in his own inimitable way, with a quirky humour and lack of pedantry that his students must at first have found quite incomprehensible. There was always something unexpected, a poetic inspiration that probably few of his students could appreciate. For example, he identified himself with the Romantic poets so much that he once declared to Shônosuke Shinki, 'I am Wordsworth, and you are Coleridge!'

The first editions of Blyth's four volumes of haiku translations and commentaries, published between 1949 and 1952 by Hokuseido, contain dedications to influential people like the Governor of the Bank of Japan, and they were financed by the then Prime Minister, Shigeru Yoshida. Blyth had the lucky gift of being able to make friends with prominent men in all walks of Japanese life — in politics, finance, education, religion and publishing; without the support of such people even the most gifted foreigner cannot expect much consideration in Japan. Yet he was definitely a man of the people, and no snob, though he may have felt tempted to be one, for one of his students saw, pinned to the wall of his study, this motto: 'Not to be sentimental. Not to be cruel. Not to be selfish. Not to be snobbish.' One does not give oneself that kind of admonition without some reason.

He was sincere and outspoken. At one summer seminar in Odawara, where nearly all the participants were Buddhists, the subject of one of his lectures bore the typically provocative title, 'Why I hate Buddhism'. He explained this disconcerting statement by saying he hated anything ending in 'ism' because an 'ism' rejects all opinions but its own, and tries to force them upon everyone. The same could be said of words ending in 'ianity'. Blyth's own religion was eclectic. His Buddhism was extremely individual, always surprising, in the true spirit of Zen. Christmas Humphries, who met Blyth several times in Japan and later became President of the British Buddhist Society, was a great admirer of his work.

Blyth loved music so much he was often moved to tears when listening to Bach or Chopin. Poetry, too, could make him weep, even as he was reading it aloud to his students. He told them, 'I often start crying when I contemplate a landscape at sunset, and think of my dear mother living all alone in England.' In 1954 he wanted to return to Britain to see her for the last time, but was prevented by the severe Japanese currency restrictions then in force. This act of unfeeling bureaucracy caused him great sorrow. He despised honours, but accepted a D. Litt. from Tokyo University for his *Zen in English Literature* and his four volumes of haiku commentaries. The government that had refused to allow him to go home to see his dying mother awarded him the Zuihôshô (Order of Merit) Fourth Grade. In order to be allowed to wear this he had to apply, through the British Embassy in Tokyo, for permission from the Queen, and he was overjoyed when this was granted, seeing it as a mark of forgiveness for his pacifism and appreciation of his work for peace and understanding between nations.

In October, 1964, Blyth had to enter the Seiroka Hospital in Tokyo, but then was moved to Shinjuku Seiwa Hospital which had a special neurological unit. He was suffering from pneumonia, and was hoping to go to Hawaii to convalesce, but a brain tumour was diagnosed, and the journey was too dangerous to be undertaken. He died on October 28.

As his home was rather far away, in Ôiso, the funeral ceremony, in the Zen Buddhist ritual he had always desired, was performed in the Old Library of Gakushûin University. He was given his last resting-place in the beautiful cemetery of Tôkeiji Temple in Kamakura, where he is surrounded by the remains of many famous philosophers, teachers and writers, including Tetsuzô Tanikawa, who lies beside him, and his old friend and spiritual guide, Daisetz Suzuki ('He who taught me not to teach' and 'He who taught me all that I don't know', as two of his significant dedications put it) who lies just below him.

Blyth's poem *Mortality* opens thus:

> We that change,
> Hate change.
> And we that pass,
> Love what abides.

It ends:

> Ashes,
> Darkness,
> Dust.

Daisetz Suzuki would have approved those chaste words and austere sentiments. That 'inner destiny' had been fulfilled.

Part 2: The Work

I first became aware of the works of Blyth in 1952 or 1953, when I held the Gregory Fellowship in Poetry at the University of Leeds. It was also a time when I was discovering Chinese and Japanese poetry and philosophy, and reading books on Zen Buddhism that were beginning to proliferate in those days, and to have a certain influence on the Beat poets of America, whom I barely knew, though I had heard of Ginsberg, Jack Kerouac and the City Lights poets. I was also reading the works of Daisetz Suzuki and Alan Watts, the gurus of the Beat Generation.

I do not know how I came into possession of Blyth's four books of haiku translations and commentaries, though I do recall I had requested them from Leeds Central Library, whose surly librarian, John Braine, demanded to know what I wanted with 'such rubbish' — an attitude to haiku which unfortunately still persists. Certainly Blyth's books were not available in W.H.Smith's. I may have picked them up at one of the shops specializing in such arcane forms of poetry outside the British Museum.

Soon I realized that these books are made for inspired dipping. I remember my enchantment on first opening *Eastern Culture* and finding the beautiful

11

chapter on *Oriental Art and Haiku*. The relationships between poetry and art and poetry and music were subjects that were then occupying my mind, and in this first encounter with Blyth I found many answers to my problems:

> The relation of oriental art to haiku is a very deep one. It is direct, in so far as a haiku poet may express his understanding pictorially as well as verbally, and the resultant haiku and haiga stand side by side on the same scrap of paper. It is indirect, in that the pictures he sees teach him how to look at and feel and listen to the world of nature [ ] so that he may say in words what the pictures say in lines, concerning that mysterious interplay of the simple and the complicated, the general and the particular.

I who was trying to write poetry about all kinds of painters from all periods — to the general disapproval of ignorant reviewers — found these simple words refreshing and illuminating. I began to look at oriental art with a completely different eye, and a new understanding. But even more delightful to me was the fact that Blyth went on to illustrate his points with references to English painters I knew and loved — Richard Wilson, Gainsborough, Constable, Cozens, Girtin, Moreland, Cotman and Crome. It was only when he had made complete contact with his English reader in this way that Blyth proceeded to introduce Chinese painters of the Tang and Sung periods, showing how in Sesshū and Hakuin Zenji there is something in oriental art that does not appear in Japanese poetry until the advent of Bashô. Then he quoted Bashô's famous haiku, the first I had read:

> On a withered branch,
> A crow is perched,
> In the autumn evening.

This was a complete picture, an ink-painting in words, with a peculiar visual and literary resonance in its apparently banal words. The resonance came, I realized, from the simple fact that someone had bothered to look at what most people would ignore as a too-obvious, ordinary scene from daily life, and to find in the flash of that haiku glance an unforgettable image.

I kept on dipping into my four books, generously illustrated by poem-paintings and painted poems, and I was absolutely entranced. The enchantment came from my apprehension that I was in the presence of a deeply cultivated mind that yet bore its remarkable learning very lightly, did not show off its scholarship, but really treated his subject with affectionate familiarity not devoid of a quirky wit. I could hear the man's voice coming to me from the printed page, a voice both bluff and quiet, common-sensical

12

yet eloquent, plain yet musical.

Later in my dippings, I was to discover that Blyth used the same technique in analyzing haiku, first comparing examples of that difficult art with familiar English poems, with passages from the Bible, with classical epigrams, with sentences from the great philosophers. I realized that while I was learning about haiku I was also taking in a great deal of knowledge about literature and philosophy — not only English, but also Chinese, Arabic, European and American authors were quoted and compared with what I could see quite clearly were their Japanese equivalents.

Blyth's books came to represent for me a compendium of Japanese culture. He discusses Nô, flower arrangement and the tea ceremony, finding in them an art of living not found in the West: 'The truth is that the East knows how to live, but does not do it; the West does not know.' He illustrates that revealing aphorism with an unexpected juxtaposed quotation from D.H. Lawrence, one of his revered authors:

> Life and love are life and love, a bunch of violets is a bunch of violets, and to drag in the idea of a point is to ruin everything. Live and let live, love and let love, and follow the natural curve, which flows on, pointless.

There could be no better illustration of the Way of Zen, and through Zen of the Way of Haiku, and Blyth had found it, not in an oriental, but in a fellow-Englishman. It is this kind of juxtaposition that constantly surprises and delights us in all Blyth's works. He pays tribute to the element of contradiction in all human life: we are all Zen Buddhists without knowing it. Blyth points out, in his marvellous little chapter on *Contradiction*, that 'In the Bible and elsewhere, these contradictions are applied to the great problems of human life'. As in certain aspects of Zen and in certain haiku. He goes on to illustrate his theme with quotations from the scriptures, from Edward Lear, Blake, Keats, Meister Eckhart, *Alice in Wonderland*, Matthew Arnold, Traherne, Thoreau, Coleridge, Browning, all mixed up with oriental poems and philosophical sayings, comparing Issa's *Plum blossoms:/ My spring / Is an ecstasy* with Browning's *God's in his Heaven;/ All's right with the world.*

> The truth is not between the two, or an alternation of them; the truth is the very contradiction itself.

True art does not reside in an artificial consistency, and he quotes Emerson's famous dictum: 'Consistency is the hobgoblin of little minds.' He might have added, from another of his best-loved poets, Whitman: 'Do I contradict myself? Very well then, I contradict myself, I am large, I contain multitudes.'

Reading R. H. Blyth is a continual voyage of discovery, not only of haiku and world literature in general, but of oneself. He gently strips away our pride, our illusions, our ignorance, and presents the world afresh to us, as if through reading we had sloughed an old skin and rediscovered the innocent curiosity of childhood. Blyth, like all the great poets and painters and musicians he loved, contains continents — but also an infinity of small, undiscovered treasure islands. In this brief account I can only hint at the quality of his writing and the beauty and soaring intelligence of his mind. It is for you, reader, to start dipping into Blyth as I did, letting your fancy guide you through these representative pages of his oeuvre which have now been culled for you so carefully from a vast mass of writing, sometimes uneven in interest, but always individual, eccentric, sensitive, playful, concerned, entertaining and instructive. I wish you, in reading Blyth, the realization I had of the poverty of my own mind, and the joy of finding at last someone who could mend all the gaps in my knowledge of literature, language and life. For to read Blyth is to enjoy that wonderful experience of finding a new ally, and to enter into an enduring friendship.

James Kirkup
Andorra, 1993

1

BLYTH'S 'AUTOBIOGRAPHY'

(This modest description of his life was written by Blyth early in 1957, when he was just short of 60 years of age. It appears in the Preface to 'Japanese Life and Character in Senryu'.)

When I look back at my one and only life I find that I was led by my inner destiny to pass through certain phases, which however were not mutually exclusive, and indeed have all persisted strongly to the present time. I began with an inborn animism, the origin of all Wordsworth's poetry, and then passed rather naturally to vegetarianism, which was or should have been one of the bases of Buddhism. By a fortunate chance I then came across haiku, or to speak more exactly *Haiku no Michi*, the Way of Haiku, which is the purely poetical (non-emotional, non-intellectual, non-moral, non-aesthetic) life in relation to nature. Next, the biggest bit of luck of all, Zen, through the books of D.T. Suzuki. Zen is what we hear in the music of Bach, which tells us that all things, including pain and death, that is, annihilation, come from the *loving* hands of God. Last but not least there appeared senryu, which might well be dignified by the term *Senryu no Michi*, the Way of Senryu, for it is an understanding of all things by laughing or smiling at them, and this means forgiving all things, ourselves and God included. It is strange that animism, vegetarianism, haiku, Zen, and senryu should blend so easily and comfortably, and there seems to be something oddly right too about their chronological order.

(In extension of this, Blyth sets out his religious beliefs in two passages — the first from 'Zen and Zen Classics', Vol. 2, and the second again from 'Japanese Life and Character in Senryu'.)

1) The other day someone asked me what my religion was.[ ] I said: 1. I believe in things, or rather, I believe things. 2. These things are all equally (but also more or less, according to internal and external circumstances) vivid, lively, life-having, life-giving, 'alive'. 3. The urge of (my own) life is to get closer and closer to things. 4. The closer we get the farther we feel, and the greater the anguish of separation. The first is Zen; the second, animism; the third, mysticism; the fourth, existentialism.

2) Religion is what D. H. Lawrence calls 'setting the little life in the circle of the greater life'; it is sweeping a room as if sweeping the universe; it is paring your nails as if your life depended on it; it is winding up your watch just before you are executed.

2

THE SONG OF ENLIGHTENMENT

(In Volume One of 'Zen and Zen Classics', Blyth answers the question, What is Zen?, and traces the history of Zen from 1000 B.C. to 715 A.D. He then explores some of the great treatises on Zen: the Hsinhsinming, the Chengtaoke (Song of Enlightenment), and the Platform Sutra. Here we have Blyth at his most insolently, amusingly brilliant, and absolute master of his material. Haiku enthusiasts will note the connection Blyth makes between Zen brevity and haiku concision.)

[ ] The teaching of the *Chengtaoke* goes back to the *Upanishads*. All is mind, is my mind, is Mind, is My Mind. There is no such thing as I and not I, nor can the two be united. (Here Yungchia goes too far back, for the oneness of things is just as unreal as their twoness; the absolute is as non-existent as the relative; Shelley's skylark is not a blithe spirit any more than it is a bird.) Further, nothing is to be chosen, nothing rejected. Whitman here agrees with him, and there is something of Blake too about Yungchia, even in his faults, for example a somewhat abusive and self-satisfied manner. We feel a desire for the modesty and self-abnegation of Ryōkan or Goldsmith.

The 'poem' is not very poetical, even in the original, if I am any judge of it. As Nietzsche says, the more abstract the doctrine, the more we must attract the senses to it. Yungchia does this, but his talking of the 'flaming Vajra blade', and 'Dharma-thunder', and 'the mani-jewel', does not appeal to the Western mind,— except to those romantic people who just like anything gorgeous and exotic. In addition, the poem is too long. Any poem is too long to express Zen, yet on the other hand, length is no obstacle to Zen, so that what is wrong is not that it consists of two hundred and seventy lines of seven characters each, but that Yungchia keeps talking when he has nothing more to say; that he is enjoying himself, not thinking of the reader too. The following are what I think to be the most important, the most unforgettable passages of the *Chengtaoke*, besides the eight quoted already in reference to the *Hsinhsinming*. It begins like this:

DO YOU NOT SEE HIM
THE REALLY WISE MAN, ALWAYS AT EASE
UNMOVED
HE DOES NOT GET RID OF ILLUSION, NOR

DOES HE SEEK FOR THE [SO-CALLED] TRUTH.
IGNORANCE IS INTRINSICALLY THE BUDDHA
NATURE
OUR ILLUSORY UNREAL BODY IS THE COSMIC
BODY.

The 'really wise man' is Bach at the organ; Bashô when he heard the frog jump into the always silent water; Eckhart when he said just before his death, 'Where to us God shows least he is often most'; Po Chü-i when he bought the hens from the butcher and released them; Mrs. Gamp when she put her lips to the gin-bottle; the three sisters Elsie, Lacie, and Tillie in the treacle well, learning to draw a 'muchness'; Mozart bursting into tears as he sings his own requiem; Wordsworth and his sister Dorothy gazing with 'joy' at the glow-worm.

The violent activity, the silent intentness, the talking, the tender-heartedness, the greediness, the nonsense, the unutterable grief, the utterable joy, —these are enlightenment.

WHEN WE ATTAIN REALITY, IT IS SEEN TO
BE NEITHER
PERSONAL NOR IMPERSONAL.

Love is not of the body, nor of the spirit, nor of a combination of the two. Poetry in the same way is the abstract and general seen in the concrete and particular; poetry is the absolute-relative, the general-particular.

Shall I call thee Bird
Or but a wandering Voice?

Reality is not the question nor the answer, but in the pause between the two. 'My Kingdom is not of this world' of cause and effect.

THERE IS NO SIN, NO PARADISE, NO LOSS
OR GAIN;
ABOUT THIS TRANSCENDENTALITY,
NO QUESTIONS!

We see good and bad, ugly and beautiful here and there, then and now, pain and pleasure,—only to go onwards (backwards) to the Undifferentiated. But this is not without differentiation. There is no bad; all things are good; some are better.

WHO IS THOUGHT-LESS? WHO IS BIRTH-LESS?

One day I received a letter from D.T.Suzuki. On the envelope[1] was written, Buraisu. This has three meanings. First, it is Blyth written in Chinese characters. Second, it means, 'You have not come to see me for a long time (not come person)'. Third, it means, 'You are a not-coming, not-going, not-born, not-dying person; you are Mr. Time-less Blyth'.

HE ALWAYS WALKS BY HIMSELF, SAUNTERS BY HIMSELF.

When people agree with me I always feel that I must be wrong.
(Oscar Wilde)
Most friendship is feigning, most loving mere folly.
(Shakespeare)
Would ye not watch with me one hour? (Christ)

Even so this happy Creature of herself
Is all-sufficient; solitude to her
Is blithe society.

O solitude, what are the charms
That sages have seen in thy face?

FROM THE TIME I RECOGNISED THE ROAD
TO TSAO-CHI,
I REALISED I HAD NOTHING TO DO WITH
BIRTH AND DEATH.

There is a line of a poem about Saint Bridget that always sticks in my mind:

St. Bridget, she loved not the world.

The universe is birth and death, birth and death; eat and be eaten; kill and be killed. If we have nothing to do with birth and death, what shall we deal with? There is something inside birth-and-death, something which is not a thing, something which is not separate or separable from it; which is identical with it and yet not it,—or is this all mystification and nonsense? When it is said or written down in words, in cold blood, we get only lifeless paradoxes. Anecdotes are better, but gradually cheapen with use, for what is true is true only once.

---

[1] *This envelope has been included in our back cover design.*

WALKING IS ZEN, SITTING IS ZEN
TALKING OR SILENT, MOVING, UNMOVING,—
ESSENCE IS AT EASE.

To realise that religion is eating, that every mouthful is the flesh of Christ, that when we walk we walk with Christ's legs, when we sit we sit with His buttocks,—this knowledge is the most exhilarating thing in the world. Every smell is the smell of God, every death is the death of God,—to know this is indeed to be at ease.

ENTERING THE DEEP MOUNTAINS
I LIVE IN QUIET SOLITUDE.
THE HILLS ARE HIGH, THE VALLEYS DEEP
WHEN ONE LIVES BENEATH AN OLD PINE-TREE.

As with the Bible, commentators symbolise away the meaning of these lines, and say that it refers to a mind that is at peace on a battlefield, and calm when engaged in making or losing millions on the stock-market. This is a convenient explanation for those who want to have the best of both worlds, but I would like to take it quite literally, and say further that the ideal world is one which is sprinkled with a limited number of poetical Robinson Crusoes (and Mrs Crusoes and little Crusoes; Mrs. Crusoe may well be a black woman Friday). Only a world of such people could be peaceful. If people are going to become successful business men by Zen, Miyamoto Musashi-like murderers by Zen, then let us have nothing to do with Zen.

WE GET RID OF ILLUSION AND ACQUIRE THE TRUTH,
BUT THIS IS DISCRIMINATION; OUR MIND IS
CLEVERLY FALSE.

Perhaps it would be better to avoid the truth like the plague, and embrace every error we come across. We should try to lose our self-control, nurse our grievances, sit doing nothing at all, be filthy, and steal the blind beggar's coins, go to bull-fights, read the newspapers.

ALL PRINCIPLES ARE NO PRINCIPLES;
THEY HAVE NO RELATION TO SPIRITUAL
PERCEPTION.

This reminds us of how D. H. Lawrence, when confronted by the 'facts' of evolution, put his hands on his solar plexus and said, 'I don't feel it here!' Whether there really is such a physico-spiritual organ as the intuition is not perhaps possible to determine, but human beings would not be human without it.

> IT NEVER LEAVES THIS PLACE, AND IS
> ALWAYS PERFECT.
> WHEN YOU LOOK FOR IT, YOU FIND YOU
> CAN'T SEE IT.
> YOU CAN'T GET AT IT,YOU CAN'T BE RID
> OF IT.
> WHEN YOU DO NEITHER, THERE IT IS!
> WHEN YOU ARE SILENT, IT SPEAKS; WHEN
> YOU SPEAK, IT IS SILENT.

'It' is always at this moment, never past or future. It never rests, even on the Seventh Day. It is like Herbert's orange tree, 'that busy plant'. How could this mechanical world of cause and effect produce such a contradictory, paradoxical thing? As Thoreau says, the tragedy begins when we try to explain ourselves; that is, the universe.

3

THE PALE CAST OF THOUGHT

(From 'Zen in English Literature and Oriental Classics'.)

The intellect has suffered a good deal of abuse at the hands of writers of all kinds. Hamlet, as befits a poet, speaks slightingly of the pure intellect:

> There are more things in Heaven and Earth, Horatio,
> Than are dreamt of in your philosophy.

Fitzgerald has his famous lines:

> Myself when young did eagerly frequent
> Doctor and Saint, and heard great argument
> About it and about: but evermore
> Came out by the same Door as in I went,

which many no doubt have tested and approved in experience: even Bacon says in his essay *Of Goodness,*

> The desire of power in excess caused the angels to fall; the desire of knowledge in excess caused man to fall.

Both Keats and Wordsworth agree that science is the arch-enemy of poetry. In *Lamia,* Keats says,

> There was an awful rainbow once in heaven;
> We know her woof, her texture; she is given
> In the dull catalogue of common things.
> Philosophy will clip an Angel's wings.

Wordsworth, in *A Poet's Epitaph,*

> Physician art thou?—one, all eyes,
> Philosopher!—a fingering slave,
> One that would peep and botanize
> Upon his mother's grave ?

and in *The Tables Turned,*

> Our meddling intellect
> Mis-shapes the beauteous forms of things:—
> We murder to dissect.
>
> Enough of science and of art;
> Close up these barren leaves;
> Come forth, and bring with you a heart
> That watches and receives,

berates the intellect soundly. Newman in *The Dream of Gerontius* goes so far as to say

> It is the very energy of thought
> Which keeps thee from thy God;

but no one has equalled Blake in his denunciations of Reason. His vocabulary is very peculiar and misleading, but if we read the following passages from *Jerusalem,* we can understand his use of 'intellect' meaning the poetic imagination:

> I know of no other Christianity and of no other Gospel than the liberty both of body and mind to exercise the Divine Arts of Imagination. What is the Divine Spirit? Is the Holy Ghost any other than an Intellectual Fountain?
> What are all the gifts of the Gospel? Are they not all mental gifts? What is the life of Man but Art and Science?
>
> I care not whether a man is Good or Evil, all that I care
> Is whether he is a Wise man or a Fool. Go! put off Holiness,
> And put on Intellect.
>
> For a Tear is an Intellectual thing.
> But the Spectre, like a hoar frost and a mildew, rose over
> Albion,
> Saying: I am God, O Sons of Men! I am your Rational
> Power!
> Am I not Bacon and Newton and Locke, who teach Humility,
> to Man,
> who teach Doubt and Experiment?
>
> He can never be a friend to the Human Race who is the preacher of Natural Morality or Natural Religion.

I will not Reason and Compare: my business is to Create.
This is the Spectre of Man, the Holy Reasoning Power.

This Reasoning Power is 'a murderer of every Divine Member', in that it takes the life from every object by abstracting the Relative qualities in which every object exists, and makes a dead thing of it.

The Zen expression for intellection is 'grasses' or 'briars and wisterias'. Blake's expression is similar:

Reasonings like vast Serpents
Enfold around my limbs, bruising my minute articulations....
I turn my eyes to the Schools and Universities of Europe,
And there behold the Loom of Locke whose Woof rages dire,
Washed by the Water-wheels of Newton: cruel Works
Of many Wheels I view, wheel without wheel, with cogs tyrannic,
Moving by compulsion each other.

The Reason, or Spectre of man, is the state of the ordinary man bound hand and foot by the contraries under which we perceive the world; the Mind, Blake calls Humanity, in the following, descriptive of the moment when a man becomes free of life-death, gain-loss, here-there.

Each Man is in his Spectre's power
Until the arrival of that hour,
When his Humanity awake
And cast his Spectre into the Lake.

All this begins to make one think there must be something good about the rational power, if it can stir up such indignation. It is hard for a rich man to enter into the Kingdom of Heaven, but it is also hard for a fool. Is it a coincidence that Christ and Buddha had extremely powerful and subtle intellects? Christ could quibble with the best of the Jewish Sophists, when necessary. And when we consider the case of Blake himself, is it not a fact, that, despite his mysticism and poetry and painting, his chief defect was, not being a genius or mad, but that he was a bit of a fool ? To paint pictures which everyone can understand, and write poems which nobody can make head or tail of without an answer book, argues lack of ordinary foresight. We do not find people like Inge or Shaw despising the reasoning faculty, because they have it. The essence of it is, of course, the power of comparison and the power of self-criticism. It is the scissors and pruning hook of the mind, without which no work of art, in its symmetric perfection, can be produced. Blake himself illustrates this in, for example, the composition of such a poem as the *Tiger* (see the Oxford *Blake*, pages 85-88) with all the different drafts and alternatives. This is a parable of our own lives, and the relation of the intellect to Zen. Just as

> The law was our schoolmaster to bring us unto Christ,

so the intellect leads us to Zen.

We are not extortioners, unjust, adulterers, even as other men. We fast twice a week, give tithes of all we possess. We read the sacred books, pray to God, repent of our sins. Yet something annoying happens, some trifling danger arises, and we find, *on thinking it over afterwards*, that however qualified we may be for playing golden harps before God Almighty, we do not know how to deal with importunate beggars, impudent servants, insolent officials, the haggling vegetable man, being pushed in and out of tram-cars, all the hundred and one trivialities of life *in this world.* The intellect it is which compares our real and ideal actions, which tells us we are not happy when we suppose we are, which reminds us that our past painful experiences are our most valuable possessions, if only we know how to use them.

> a comfort seemed to touch
> A heart that had not been disconsolate:
> Strength came where weakness was not known to be.
> *(Prelude, IV,*153.)

To be ungrateful to your own intellect is just as bad as ingratitude to a benefactor. The only thing is, the intellect must not be divided from the energy of the personality and work in vacuo, or as a substitute for the activity of the person as a whole. *But it is the intellect which reminds us of this.* The intellect is sometimes spoken of as raising problems. It does nothing of the sort. Life raises the problems; disease, accident, violence without, greed, laziness, cruelty within, give us our daily, hourly examination. We fail; and it is the intellect which tells us so, which points to the problems, sorts and arranges them, ticks off those we have successfully solved.

After giving the intellect its due we can now define its limitations. There are three ways in which the intellect over-reaches itself.

1. It usurps the function of religion, in supposing it can understand life. The intellect can understand intellectual things; life can understand living things. But they cannot understand each other, so long as they are apart. Ikkyû says we cannot find out how the flowers grow by cutting open a tree;

> Tear open the tree !

And can you see
The cherry flowers that yearly
Bloom on Yoshino ?

Emerson has a similar thought in *Each and All:*

I wiped away the weeds and foam,
I fetched my sea-born treasures home;
But the poor, unsightly, noisome things
Had left their beauty on the shore,
With the sun and the sand and the wild uproar.

We see the necessity for that immediacy which Zen insists on, and which is not the characteristic of the intellect. The intellect is a collector.

2. It usurps the function of poetry when it replaces the imagination, the compassion, of the poet. It is particularly detestable in, for example, Tennyson's

Faith hears the lark within the songless egg.

One would like to read some lines on a maiden asleep on a pillow stuffed with the feathers of the lark which would have come out of the egg, only someone ate it. This is not poetry at all. It is a kind of proleptic vivisection. We get the same thing in the last two lines of the first verse of *The Palm Willow* of Robert Bridges.

See whirling snow sprinkles the starved field,
The birds have stayed to sing;
No covert yet their fairy harbour yields
When cometh Spring?
Ah! in their tiny throats what songs unborn
Are quenched each morn.

A similar case, in the human world, is Davies'

Sweet Poesy, why art thou dumb?
I fear thy singing days are done;
The poet in my soul is dying,
And every charm in life is gone.

When a poet begins to talk like this, he is finished, done for, dead. Intellection, as in the later Wordsworth, replaces imagination, and imagination, which is the becoming one with the thing contemplated, has no connection with the thing contemplated, has no connection with the mere desire to write verses.

Two examples from early haiku follow:

Kakka eda ni kaeru to mireba kachô kana
A fallen flower
Flew back to its branch!
No, it was a butterfly.   *Moritake*

Gaikotsu no ue o yosôte hanami kana
Their skeletons wrapt
In silk and satin,
They view the cherry blossoms.   *Onitsura*

Of the first we may say that poetry should deal with facts, not mistakes or optical illusions; whether the things concerned are beautiful or not does not affect the question. And of the second, human beings are only skeletons, it is true, and silk and satin only rags, but cherry blossoms are only little flat pieces of coloured pulp.

3. Last, the intellect is guilty of constructing dogmas, systems of philosophy, which imprison the mind, until it mopes like a monkey in a cage. In *Empedocles on Etna*, Arnold speaks of the two enemies of life, of Zen;

Some bondage of the flesh or mind,
Some slough of sense, or some fantastic maze
Forged by the imperious lonely thinking power.

'Maze' is the right word for the history of philosophy. 'Fantastic' is justly applied to what leaves out of account life itself. 'Forged' shows its mechanical nature; 'imperious', the dreadful intensity of the destructive analysis.'Lonely' is interesting. Emotion may be communicated in a variety of ways, it is infectious. Thought is peculiarly individual, communicable only in words, and establishing barriers between the fool and the sage where emotions unite. Nothing divides men so much as thought.

It is true, in a way, to say that Zen may belong to the warrior, to the priest, to the pimp, to the Christian, to the atheist, to the fanatic, to the animal, to the saint; yet from another point of view it is not so, for, though Zen leaves a man free to believe in any doctrines, to perform any actions, in its relation to our beliefs it demands that we distinguish the essential from the inessential. What is the essential? Zen is the only essential. What is inessential? All the rest, especially the emotional and intellectual rubbish that hinders our freedom. Just as

> Perfect love casteth out fear,

so true Zen casts out every kind of bondage, which includes fear.
Freedom is perfect, pure freedom, but Milton said of liberty,

> For who loves that must first be wise and good.

Freedom means freedom from error and superstition, freedom to be good.
The more freedom, the more truth; the more truth, the more freedom,—this
is a natural law everywhere demonstrated in the history of human thought.
Thus the construction of dogmatic beliefs by the highest intellect reduces
man to the same state of mental slavery as the crudest and most infantile
superstition. The philosopher and the savage are just as distant from the truth.
Nevertheless, as pointed out above, while there's intellect, there's hope.
False and unfounded notions, impossible romantic illusions may be destroyed with the help of the very intellect which helped to create them.

If the intellect then is simply a vacuum-cleaner, there is nothing to do but
rely upon instinct. Emerson accepts this alternative, saying, in *Nature*,

> If the single man plant himself indomitably on his instincts, and there
> abide, the huge world will come round to him.

Zen also says we are to act self-lessly, thought-lessly, instinctively, taking
no thought, not only for the morrow, but for today, for the present as well.
So be it, but what instinct are we to follow? Shall we follow them all as they
arise in their wild confusion? And if we distinguish between them, the
resulting action can no longer be called instinctive. The Mind is not what
William James, in criticism of Hegel's *Absolute,* called 'block Reality'. It is
alive, and in the temporal process of becoming vegetable, animal, conscious,
self-conscious, many instincts have arisen and fixed themselves almost
incurably on the human mind. What Zen wishes to do is to take us back to
the most primitive condition of all, to lead us to become, not only children,
but foetuses, amoebae. Santayana is therefore quite correct when he writes
(contemptuously) of Mysticism in the last chapter of the *Life of Reason:*

> Mysticism is the most primitive of feelings and only visits formed
> minds in moments of intellectual arrest and dissolution. It can exist
> in a child, very likely in an animal; indeed, to parody a phrase of
> Hegel's, the only pure mystics are brutes.

Wordsworth says the same thing, only complimentarily:

Fallings from us, vanishings
Blank misgivings of a creature
Moving about in worlds not realised,
High instincts before which our mortal nature
Did tremble like a guilty thing surprised.

What is this fundamental instinct, this ground of being which Zen wishes us to reach? Freud tells us it is sex, and Zen will not wish to dispute this. *Satori* [1] is a spiritual orgasm. The sexual orgasm is a physical reunion, the primitive instinct arising from the separation of cell from cell, of the animal from its young. It is temporary, recurrent, causing immediate relief and absence of desire, leading to self-reliance and self-realisation.

The spiritual orgasm is a spiritual reunion of Man and God. It has no reaction, is not under control, coming and going like the wind; it leads to self-lessness. It causes a far more fundamental change of attitude to the outside world. [   ]

---

[1] *satori, often translated as 'enlightenment', the end and aim of Zen life, gives man a new viewpoint, a new way of seeing the ordinary things of life. It cannot be taught, it must be sought without strain, and found by each individual himself (or herself).*

4

BASHÔ

(From 'Haiku', Vol. 1, Section 4.)

There are three great names in the history of haiku, Bashô, Buson and Issa; we may include a fourth, Shiki. Bashô is the religious man, Buson the artist, Issa the humanist. Bashô is concerned with God as he sees himself in the mind of the poet before flowers and fields. Buson deals with things as they exist by and for themselves, in their own right. Issa is concerned with man, man the weak angel; with birds and beasts as they struggle like us to make a living and keep their heads above water. If we do not begin with Bashô, our interpretation of haiku is bound to lack depth. The objectivity of Buson and the subjectivity of Issa both spring from the homely little man with long eyebrows and a bad digestion.

It is truer in Japanese poetry than in any other, that for the understanding of it we need to understand the poet. Jinsai Itô [1] said,

> Where the teacher is, there is truth; respect for the teacher is respect for truth.

When therefore we come to Bashô, we do so because he is the Way, the Truth and the Life. Apart from human beings, there is no Buddha. Nevertheless, there is to be no imitation of Christ or any other person, no imitation of any teacher. In Bashô's own words,

> Do not follow in the footsteps of the Ancients; seek what they sought.

As with Wordsworth, piety was the foundation of both Bashô's character and of his literary work. To him more than to any other oriental poet do Gensei's [2] words apply;

> By making faithfulness and filial piety the fundamental, and giving literary work a secondary place, poetry is profound.

We may compare what Wordsworth says:

> To be incapable of a feeling of poetry, in my sense of the word, is to be without love of human nature and reverence for God.

---

[1] *1627-1705, Confucianist scholar*   [2] *1623-96, priest and tanka poet.*

Bashô felt that life was not deep enough, not continuous enough, and he wanted to give every action, every moment the value that it potentially had. He wanted the little life we lead to be at the same time the greater life. Every flower was to be the spring, every pain a birth pang, every man a haiku poet, walking in the Way of Haiku.

> It was the life of the little day, the life of little people. And the man who had died said to himself, 'Unless we encompass it in the greater day, and set the little life in the circle of the greater life, all is disaster.[1]

What is this greater life, and how is the little life to be related to it? Or, to put the question in a more prosaic but more pertinent form, what is the social value of haiku? When we compare the life of Bashô especially, or of any other great haiku poet, with those of Wordsworth, Milton, Shelley, Keats, and so on, we are struck by one fact of seemingly little importance, that the Japanese haiku poets all had disciples; the English poets none. This is a matter of the greatest significance, for it is just here, in this religious attitude, that the little, prosaic life of little people may be set in the greater, the poetic life.

> *Fuyu-gomori mata yorisowan kono hashira*
> Winter seclusion:
> Once again I will lean against
> This post.   *Bashô*

Here, and here only, is the little life set in the circle of the greater, the ordinary in the extraordinary, the commonplace in the miraculous, the material in the spiritual, the human in the divine. To sit on the floor and lean one's back against a post may not seem the acme of comfort, but this is the pleasure Bashô is promising himself. During the winter, while the snow is silently falling, he will lean against the post as he did last year, reading and writing poetry, thinking

> Thoughts that wander through eternity,

through *our* eternity, through the greater life. This post rubbed smooth with countless vigils, black where his head rested against it, is all he asks for.

The Way of Haiku requires not only a Franciscan poverty, but this concentration of all the energies of mind and body, a perpetual sinking of oneself into things. Bashô tells us, and it is to be noted, we believe him:

[1] Lawrence, *The Man Who Died.*

Meigetsu ya ike o megurite yo mo sugara
The autumn full moon:
All night long
I paced round the lake.

All night gazing at the moon, and only this poor verse to show for it? But it must be remembered that Bashô was a teacher. And thus we too, when we look at the moon, look at it with the eyes of Bashô, those eyes that gazed at that moon and its reflection in the placid water of the lake. Buson says,

Samushiro o hatake ni shiite ume-mi kana
Spreading a straw mat in the field,
I sat and gazed
At the plum blossoms.

This sitting and looking at a flowering tree is not quite so simple and easy as it appears. Buson, besides being a poet, was an artist, and was expressing in silence and motionlessness the poetic and artistic meaning of this plum tree (for this is the meaning of 'gazing'). One of Bashô's haiku which illustrates both this plain severity of life and his tender affection for his pupils is the following:

Haru tatsu ya aratoshi furuki kome goshô
The beginning of spring:
For the new year,
Five-*shô* of rice from last year.

At Fukagawa, Bashô's disciples, especially Sampû, brought him all the necessities of life. He had in the house a large gourd which would hold five *shô* (1 *shô* = 3.18 pints = 1.8 litres). The happiness of the New Year is the remembrance of the fidelity and affection of his pupils, symbolized in the rice remaining over from the year before. A similar verse is:

Putting on a silk garment that Ransetsu gave me for the New Year

Tare yara ka sugata ni nitari kesa no haru
The first morning of spring:
I feel like
Someone else.

Literally, 'Whom do I look like?' Bashô's lack of affectation is shown also in the following:

Answering Kikaku's poem about *tade* (smart-weed) and the firefly.

> *Asagao ni   ware wa meshi kû   otoko kana*
> I am one
> Who eats his breakfast,
> Gazing at the morning-glories.

This was Bashô's reply to:

> *Kusa no to ni   ware wa tade kû   hotaru kana*
> A firefly,
> I partake of the smart-weed,
> In my hermitage.   *Kikaku*

Kikaku means that, like the firefly, he prefers the night, and has eccentric tastes, enjoying the bitter flavour of the smart-weed that other people dislike. Bashô says that the true poetic life is not here, but in eating one's rice and pickles for breakfast and gazing at whatever nature and the seasons bring us. It would be just as hard to think of Bashô living in affluence or as even moderately well-off, as it would to imagine St. Francis a rich man. Bashô lived a life very similar to that of Meg Merrilies:

> No breakfast had she many a morn,
> No dinner many a noon,
> And 'stead of supper she would stare
> Full hard against the Moon.

Chora gives us a picture of Bashô,—how different from that of the average European poet:

> *Tabi-sugata   shigure no tsuru yo   Bashô-ô*
> In travelling attire,
> A stork in late autumn rain:
> The old master Bashô.

The first poem in the *Nozarashi Diary* shows us Bashô's idea of the normal state of the poet, little different from that of the ascetic. The end proposed is not different from that ideal which Keats held up before himself, but the means are poles apart:

> *Nozarashi o   kokoro ni kaze no   shimu mi kana*
> Resigned to death by exposure,

How the wind
Cuts through me !

Prepared to die by the roadside, he sets out on his journey. Why did he not stop at home, if not in comfort, at least out of the wind and rain? For several reasons. **Without contact with things, with cold and hunger, real poetry is impossible.** Further, Bashô was a missionary spirit and knew that all over Japan were people capable of treading the Way of Haiku. But beyond this, just as with Christ, Bashô's heart was turned towards poverty and simplicity; it was his fate, his lot; his destiny as a poet.

> *Toshi no ichi senkô kai ni ideba yana*
> The year-end fair:
> I would like to go out and buy
> Some incense-sticks.

The modesty of Bashô's desires is evident in this verse. Nothing could be cheaper, or more cheerless, by ordinary standards. Bashô's sympathy with animate things did not arise from any theory of the unity of life, nor from an innate love of living things. It was strictly poetic, and for this reason we find it partial and limited, but sincere. It springs, as is seen in the individual cases where it is expressed, from a deep experience of a particular case. Bashô was once returning from Ise, the home of the gods, to his native place of sad memories. Passing through the lonely forest, the cold rain pattering on the fallen leaves, he saw a small monkey sitting huddled on a bough, with that submissive pathos which human beings can hardly attain to. Animals alone possess it. He said:

> *Hatsu-shigure saru mo komino o hoshige nari*
> First winter rain:
> The monkey also seems
> To want a small straw cloak.

He was preserved from any sentimentality about animals by the fact that his own life was full of discomfort, which he saw as inevitable, and, in a sense, desirable. The gentleness of Bashô (who was a samurai by birth) is a very special quality. We may perhaps compare him to Chaucer, of whom Thoreau says:

> We are tempted to say that his genius was feminine, not masculine. It was such a feminineness, however, as is rarest to find in woman, though not the appreciation of it; perhaps it is not to be found at all in woman, but is only the feminine in man.

Bashô was not a great poetical genius by birth. During the first forty years of his life he wrote no verse that could be called remarkable, or even good. Unlike his contemporary Onitsura, who was mature at twenty-five, Bashô made his way into the deepest realm of poetry by sheer effort and study, study here meaning not mere learning, but a concentration on the spiritual meaning of the culture he had inherited in haikai. Indeed, we may say that few men have been so really cultured as Bashô was, with his understanding of Confucianism, Taoism, Chinese Poetry, waka[1], Buddhism, Zen, Painting, the Art of Tea. In *Oi no Kobumi,* he writes:

> Saigyô's waka, Sôgi's renga, Sesshû's painting,
> Rikyû's Tea,—the spirit animating them is one.

Under Kigin, 1623-1705, Bashô probably studied the *Manyôshû,* the *Kokinshû,* the *Shin Kokinshû,* the *Genji Monogatari,* the *Tosa Diary,* the *Tsurezuregusa* and Saigyô's waka in his *Sankashû.* Other haiku poets also studied Saigyô, e.g. the verse of Sôin, written on a picture of Saigyô-Hôshi,

> *Aki wa kono hôshi sugata no yûbe kana*
> This Hôshi's appearance.
> In the evening,
> Is that of autumn.

There are a great number of haiku concerning Priest Saigyô, and not a few of Bashô's referring to or based on Saigyô's waka. Bashô's interest in these was due to their apparent objectivity but real subjectivity, their *yûgen,* their painful feeling, artistry, purity. More than the Chinese poets, he admired Saigyô for his life of poverty and wandering, his deep fusion of poetry and religion.

With truly Japanese genius, he did not merely read and repeat the words and phrases of these men, but put their spirit into practice in his daily life. There is a far-off but deep resemblance here between Bashô and Johnson, two utterly different types of men, who yet both hold a position in the history of literature higher than their actual writings warrant, by virtue of their personal character. When all is written that can be written, and all is done that can be done, it may be found that Bashô was not only the greatest of all the Japanese, but that he is to be numbered among those few human beings who lived, and taught us how to live by living.

---

[1] *Nowadays the term tanka is usually employed instead of waka, for the 5-line verse composed of 5-7-5-7-7 sound units.*

Bashô's verses are comparatively few in number, about two thousand in all, of which about a hundred are really good, but one thing that strikes us about them is their variety. We can see in his verses the tendencies which later poets developed.

Epic

Fukitobasu ishi wa Asama no nowaki kana
The autumn blast
Blows along the stones
On Mount Asama.

Chinoiserie

Yogi wa omoshi goten ni yuki o miru aran
The bed clothes are so heavy,
The snow of the sky of the Kingdom of Wu
Will soon be seen.

Still Life

Shio dai no haguki mo samushi uo no tana
In the fish-shop
The gums of the salted sea-bream
Are cold.

Unconventionality

No o yoko ni uma hikimuke yo hototogisu
Lead my horse
Across the moor
To where the *hototogisu* is singing!

Humour

Mugi-meshi ni yatsururu koi ka neko no tsuma
The lady-cat,
With love and barley-rice
So thin!

Picturesqueness

> *Shigururu ya ta no arakabu no kuromu hodo*
> First winter rain,—
> Enough to turn
> The stubble black.

Delicacy

> *Chimaki musubu katate ni hasamu hitai-gami*
> Wrapping rice dumplings in bamboo leaves,
> With one hand she fingers
> The hair over her forehead.

When we call Bashô the greatest of the (haiku) poets of Japan, it is not only for his creation of a new form of human experience, and the variety of his powers, illustrated above. He has an all-round delicacy of sympathy which makes us near to him, and him to us. As with Dr Johnson, there is something in him beyond literature, above art, akin to what Thoreau calls homeliness. In itself, mere goodness is not very thrilling but when it is added to sensitivity, a love of beauty, and poetry, it is the irresistible force which can move immovable things.

What was it that made Bashô suddenly realise that poetry is not beauty, as in waka, or morality, as in *dôka*, or intellectuality and verbal wit as in haikai? Some say it was the result of his study of Zen, but this seems to me very unlikely. Bashô does not seem to have urged his disciples to do *zazen*, and seldom speaks about Zen and its relation to haiku. The fact is that haiku would have come into being even if Bashô had never been born. We cannot say, however, that somebody would have written Shakespeare's plays even if Shakespeare (or Bacon, or Marlowe, or the Earl of Oxford, or Queen Elizabeth) had not. What Thoreau said, that 'Man, not Shakespeare or Homer, is the great poet', is truer of Japan than of any other country, where custom and tradition are stronger, and where the poetry was not a romantic or classical solo, but a democratic trio or quartet. Again, [   ], Onitsura, Gonsui and many lesser men were composing good haiku at the same time as Bashô. However, they did not have the modesty, the generosity, the ambitionlessness of Bashô. Onitsura loved sincerity and truth and made them his object, but Bashô just loved.

5

ISSA

(This is Chapter 20 of "History of Haiku", Vol .1)

Buson was born in 1715, twenty-one years after Bashô's death. When Buson died in 1783, Issa was twenty. Bashô influenced Buson strongly, though Buson was a shallower character, but Issa never met Buson, it seems, and was not influenced by him. The influence of Bashô of course was strong on Issa, but Bashô had a breadth of soul (not of mind) which Issa had not. Bashô's soul was like Christ's heaven, it had many mansions, he could embrace many people, and could write many kinds of haiku. Issa had no master, no real disciples. He reminds us of Swift and Burns in his solitariness, and with them wished to love, and still more to be loved, but was like Wordsworth's Matthew, 'not enough beloved'.

Issa's life is said to have been a sad one, and people speak of him with a pity that Issa would have found disagreeable, if not unexpected. When Hazlitt lay dying, he surprised everybody by saying,'I have had a happy life'. It would not be astonishing to know that Issa said the same thing on his death-bed. As Stevenson (should have) said:

> The world is so full of a number of things,
> I'm sure we should all be as happy as Issa.

Being an orphan, not having a fixed home until he was fifty, the death of a wife, children dying like flies,—these are troubles above the average, but Issa also had happiness, or rather blessedness, far above the average. He did not 'see life steadily and see it whole' like the great men that Arnold admired. He saw it unsteadily, and in its parts, but perhaps this is all that anyone can do. What distinguishes one man from another, what differentiates the real Hell from the real Heaven, is depth, and Issa felt the smallest things deeply. Breadth must always sacrifice depth. And steadiness is the attitude of the scientist and the philosopher. The chameleon poet must be as unsteady, as unpredictable as (poetical) nature, and this sameness with nature constitutes his 'happiness'.

It is not necessary to be poor to know that men are greedy and insolent. An ironic view of life comes from inside, not outside. When ideals are high, reality looks bad. A sense of humour lets us into secrets hidden from the wise and prudent. If we love living creatures, we pity ourselves in them, and them in ourselves. Bashô also was a sensitive and sympathetic poet. He loved nature, and the mind of man was for him also the main region of his song.

But his resignation, his lack of resistance to the powers that be, deprive his haiku of irony, and leave them with only the faint humour of nature that poetry can never omit. [   ]

Issa is a little like Heine in his tendency to sentimentality, and playing with motherless sparrows, his dislike of pretence (sentimentality is itself a subtle kind of pretence), his love of contrast and sarcasm. For Issa's love of living things, especially the least respectable ones, we must go to John Clare for a comparison. Issa often has Thoreau's dryness, and always his friendliness with nature. Issa could not say, as Thoreau did, that he regretted nothing, and though Issa also never quarrelled with God, he had to suppress a mutinous spirit to do so. One odd thing about Issa, mentioned before, something that should be carefully studied, is the fact that in spite of his humanity—he is in many ways the least Japanese of the haiku poets—he had very few disciples, at least good ones. One was Seifu-jo, 1783-1840, wife of Shunkô, a haiku poet. I don't know any more. Bashô, Buson, and Shiki all had many disciples, Issa practically none; what does this show? Christ is said to have had twelve, but he died alone. Bashô himself is supposed to have been speaking metaphorically when he wrote:

> *Kono michi ya yuku hito nashi ni aki no kure*
> An autumn eve;
> Along this road
> Goes no one.

But who is Bach's disciple? Certainly not his silly sons. Who is Nietzsche's? Who is Wordsworth's, or Thoreau's, or Lawrence's, or Blake's, or mine even? In this respect Bashô was an exception, a really good man. Bashô is concerned with the religious meaning of things, Buson with their beauty and strangeness, Issa with their (comical) thinginess. These trivia are at the same time felt as tragic, so that Issa is one of the great ironists. The parting of Hector and Andromache, the first kiss of Francesca da Rimini, the death of Lear,— these are more lofty, more piercing, more dreadful, but they do not come so close to our business and bosoms as do Issa's verses. John Hall, in his *A Pastorall Hymne*, says:

> Yet do the lazy Snailes no lesse
> The greatnesse of our Lord confesse.

Bashô often has the solemnity of Wordsworth. When setting out on a journey,

Tabibito to waga na yobaren hatsu-shigure
The first winter rain;
My name shall be called
'Traveller.'

Issa says:

Mukudori to hito ni yobaruru samusa kana
'Country bumpkin'
People call me,—
How cold it is!

Issa had actually lived long in Edo, but was poor, and indifferent to clothes, so they called him 'grey starling'. Thoreau has the same lack of solemnity: from his Journal, 1853:

The other day, when I had been standing perfectly still some ten minutes, looking at a willow which had just blossomed, some rods in the rear of Martial Miles's house, I felt eyes on my back and, turning round suddenly, saw the heads of two who had stolen out of the house and were watching me over a rising ground fixedly as I the willow. They were studying man, which is said to be the proper study of mankind, I nature, and yet, when detected, they felt the cheapest of the two.

The most remarkable, and to me the most delightful part of Issa's character is his love of flies and mosquitoes and so forth. Issa felt about fleas and lice what Eckhart says:

[When I preach to the people of Paris I just speak and trust that I speak well; the whole of Paris with all its arts cannot comprehend what God is in the smallest of creatures, yes, even in a midge.]

Issa can do what all Paris could not do, and what even Eckhart could not,— see a midge in God. Seeing God in a midge is not so difficult. What is really difficult is to keep one's eye fixed steadily on the insects, and not let God usurp their divinity. Issa wrote 54 haiku on the snail, 15 on the toad, nearly 200 on frogs (which belong to spring), about 230 on the firefly, more than 150 on the mosquito, 90 on flies, over 100 on fleas, nearly 90 on the cicada, and about 70 on various other insects, a grand total of about a thousand verses on such creatures. Some may say, 'Little things please little minds'. But Christ tells us that the hairs of our heads are all numbered, and Issa thought that the hairs on a hairy caterpillar were numbered. I think so too. [   ]

6

WORDSWORTH

*(Wordsworth's importance to Blyth can be judged from his list of 'great men',
which he gives in the Introduction to 'Zen and Zen Classics', Vol. 4. 'I myself
would choose,' he says, 'in this order, Bach, Bashô, Thoreau, Unmon, as the
first four, with Shakespeare, Mozart, Wordsworth, Eckhart, Po Chü-i and
others following. The order is the order of Zen.' What follows is the
penultimate chapter of 'Zen in English Literature and Oriental Classics' (the
final one is on Shakespeare).*

The change that took place in Wordsworth as he passed from Zen through
Pantheism to Orthodoxy, is almost unparalleled in the history of culture. The
three periods of course overlap, but we are able, especially in *The Prelude*
and *The Excursion*, almost to see the change taking place under our very
eyes. In his earliest years, he tells us [in the *Tintern Abbey* ode]

> The sounding cataract
> Haunted me like a passion : the tall rock,
> The mountain, and the deep and gloomy wood,
> Their colours and their forms, were then to me
> An appetite: a feeling and a love,
> *That had no need of a remoter charm,*
> By thought supplied, nor any interest
> Unborrowed from the eye.

This is the true region of haiku. Words are many and the thing is one, but
somehow it has got to be portrayed or suggested in words,—but as a unity,
not after the post-mortem of thought, not after the dissection of the intellect.
As an example of such a haiku we may take Kyorai's,

> *Ôô to iedo tataku ya yuki no mon*
> 'Yes, yes ! ' I answered,
> But someone still knocked
> At the snow-mantled gate.

or Bashô's, composed at Kyorai's house,
> *Hototogisu ôtake yabu o moru tsukiyo*
> A cuckoo cried !
> The moon filters through
> The vast bamboo grove.

Wordsworth expresses an extreme case of this thoughtless, almost senseless state, in *Personal Talk* :

> To sit without emotion, hope, or aim,
> In the loved presence of my cottage-fire,
> And listen to the flapping of the flame,
> Or kettle whispering its faint undersong.

In these lines we can see Bashô sitting in his hut at Fukagawa. Or another example, reminding one irresistibly of Bashô, the last verse of *The Two April Mornings:*

> Matthew is in his grave, yet now,
> Methinks, I see him stand,
> As at that moment, with a bough
> Of wilding in his hand.

Again, in *Strange Fits of Passion Have I Known*, Wordsworth says, as he rode towards the sinking moon,

> My horse moved on: hoof after hoof
> He raised, and never stopped:
> When down behind the cottage roof,
> At once, the bright moon dropped.
>
> What fond and wayward thoughts will slide
> Into a Lover's head!
> 'Oh mercy!' to myself I cried,
> 'If Lucy should be dead!'

Wordsworth leaves us with this mystery of the mind of man, which selects, rejects, remembers, and associates according to its own sweet will. Why did the visitor continue knocking after Kyorai had answered 'Yes, yes', and who was he, and what did he want? Why did Wordsworth's heart suddenly contract with unwarranted fear? Why did he remember Matthew at that particular moment? What was the connection between the voice of the cuckoo and the moonlight that stole through the leaves of the bamboo ? These questions are out of place when one considers that the poems are the answers to them. We can say of these poems what Wordsworth said of those men wanting the faculty of verse,

> Theirs is the language of the heavens, the power,
> The thought, the image, and the silent joy:
> Words are but under-agents in their souls.
>
> *(Prelude XIII, 270)*

They are like the sounds of the coming storm,

> notes that are
> The ghostly language of the ancient earth.
>
> *(Prel. II,* 308)

In his early years Wordsworth's one object was to live

> the life
> In common things—the endless store of things,
> Rare, or at least so seeming, every day
> Found all about me in one neighbourhood.
>
> *(Prel. I,* 108)

He perceived with almost painful distinctness the shapes and forms of the rocks and plants and clouds, and his own character was moulded

> By inward concords, silent, inobtrusive
> And gentle agitations of the mind
> From manifold distinctions, difference
> Perceived in things.
>
> *(Prel. II,* 297)

When he looked at the lake,

> the calm
> And dead still water lay upon my mind
> Even with a weight of pleasure, and the sky,
> Never before so beautiful, sank down
> Into my heart.
>
> *(Prel. II,* 170)

What he perceived was Existence, the existence of all things, animate and inanimate:

> I felt the sentiment of Being spread
> O'er all that moves and all that seemeth still.
>
> *(Prel. II,* 401)

But what he perceived was not something outside, something separated from himself. *It was almost as if the object used his eyes to perceive itself,* or as he expresses it,

> bodily eyes
> Were utterly forgotten, and what I saw

Appeared like something in myself, a dream,
A prospect in the mind.

(Prel. II, 349)

He could not find a single object in the whole universe, not a single thing

Whose truth is not a motion or a shape
Instinct with vital functions.

(Prel. VIII, 298)

All was Activity, as he looked with

an eye
Which, from a tree, a stone, a withered leaf,
To the broad ocean and the azure heavens
Spangled with kindred multitudes of stars,
Could find no surface where its power might sleep.

(Prel. III, 162)

This reminds us of the Zen simile of Truth as an iron ball which we cannot take a bite out of. The highest point in Wordsworth's youthful directness of insight into the life of Nature is contained in the famous lines from *There Was A Boy:*

Then sometimes, in that silence, while he hung
Listening, a gentle shock of mild surprise
Has carried far into his heart the voice
Of mountain-torrents; or the visible scene
Would enter unawares into his mind
With all its solemn imagery, its rocks,
Its woods, and that uncertain heaven received
Into the bosom of the steady lake.

Farther than this, in regard to Nature, no man can go; but the problem remains; how can our bosoms become as a steady lake, to receive the uncertainties of our human life? That is to say, we must turn from Nature to Man.

Wordsworth's answer to this question is thoroughly in accord with that of Zen. Zen says, Act according to your essence of mind; in the words of the Fifth Patriarch:

Perfect Enlightenment means spontaneous realisation of your
Original Nature.

Wordsworth says,

> Come forth into the light of things,
> Let Nature be your Teacher.

Zen says, Look within! Wordsworth says, Look without! but there is no more difference here than in the case of Self-Power and Other-Power. Self-Power *is* Other-Power, because Self is Other. Looking at the microcosm *is* looking at the macrocosm, for one without the other is meaningless. 'Where man is not, nature is barren'. Wordsworth makes everything moral:

> To every natural form, rock, fruit or flower
> Even the loose stones that cover the high-way
> I gave a moral life.
>
> *(Prel. III, 130)*

Zen takes away from man even that which he hath not, his morality:

> 'Forget the difference between a saint and an ordinary man!' said the Sixth Patriarch,

but here again, if you are not attached to the words, you will see the identity of the experience, a realisation of

> what an empire we inherit
> As natural beings in the strength of Nature.
>
> *(Prel. III, 195)*

Whether we ascribe morality to man and nature or not, does not matter, as long as we do not separate them qualitatively. How is it that Nature, external Nature, can teach us? Clearly, because of the continuity of the internal and external nature, so that we see

> the parts
> As parts, but with a feeling of the whole.
>
> *(Prel. VII, 735)*

As an illustration of this identity of inner and outer we have Wordsworth's beautiful lines, describing how, after spending a night in dancing, gaiety and mirth, he went out and beheld the rising of the sun, the waves dancing, the mountains shining, birds singing, labourers going forth to work:

> My heart was full: I made no vows, but vows
> Were made for me.
>
> *(Prel. IV, 334)*

44

In *The Tables Turned,* Wordsworth asserts, as from his own experience, something that has upset both the moralists and the poets:

> One impulse from a vernal wood
> May teach you more of man,
> Of moral evil and of good,
> Than all the sages can.

This is pure Zen, as we may see if we try to answer the question, 'What can a vernal wood teach us?' The answer is, 'It teaches us!' This annoys the moralist, who is at a loss without his book of words. It annoys the poet, because he does not want to be taught morality. In *The Excursion,* Book Four, Wordsworth expands this idea of the inarticulate language of animate and inanimate things. The poetic quality is low and the thought diffuse and thin, but it is worth quoting in order to attempt to convince intellectually those who have no intuition of its truth.

> For, the Man—
> Who, in this spirit, communes with the Forms
> Of nature, who with understanding heart
> Both knows and loves such objects as excite
> No morbid passions, no disquietude,
> No vengeance, and no hatred—needs must feel
> The joy of that pure principle of love
> So deeply, that, unsatisfied with aught
> Less pure and exquisite, he cannot choose
> But seek for objects of a kindred love
> In fellow-natures, and a kindred joy.

In *Ruth,* Wordsworth shows the effect of tropical nature 'to feed voluptuous thought' in a man without self-control and of vicious life, but adds, and I think justifiably,

> Yet, in his worst pursuits I ween
> That sometimes there did intervene
> Pure hopes of high intent:
> For passions linked to forms so fair
> And stately needs must have their share
> Of noble sentiment,

that is to say, even where the effect of external Nature seems only to debase, it is actually mixed with good.

Now we come to a more painful part of our study of Wordsworth, that of the gradual disintegration of his poetical character. This was partly due to an inexplicable decrease in his intuitive powers and corresponding inspiration and output of real poetry, and partly the effect of the introspection and self-analysis to which he so rigorously subjected himself. We can trace, in *The Prelude* and *The Excursion*, the growth of a pantheism, a theoretical interpretation of his original insight, which ultimately destroys him. He tells us himself that he learned

> To look on nature, not as in the hour
> Of thoughtless youth.

The division of man and nature begins when we imagine things as they ought to be, not as they are. Wordsworth records his disappointment at the sight of the actual Mont Blanc,

> and grieved
> To have a soulless image on the eye
> That had usurped upon a living thought.
>
> *(Prel. VI, 525)*

He talks of how

> An auxiliar light
> Came from my mind, which on the setting sun
> Bestowed new splendour,
>
> *(Prel. II, 368)*

This is unfortunately in accord with his (later) peculiar definitions of the Imagination. He says,

> Imagination, which, in truth,
> Is but another name for absolute power
> And clearest insight, amplitude of mind,
> And Reason in her most exalted mood.
>
> *(Prel. XIV, 189)*

This, though not very clear, one can hardly disagree with, but in a conversation, Wordsworth said,

> Imagination is a subjective term; it deals with objects not as they are, but as they appear to the mind of the poet,

and this is positively dangerous, opening the way to all kinds of capricious and fanciful creations out of all relation with truth. What Wordsworth no doubt means by 'objects as they are', is things not worked up in the mind of the perceiver, but in this sense, no such object can be represented at all. Again, in the Preface to the Edition of 1815, Wordsworth discusses at length the function of the Imagination. What he says is not so much wrong as it is detestable, as Wordsworth usually is in his later prose and poetry. He states there that Imagination is a word

> denoting operations of the mind upon those objects, and processes of creation or of composition, governed by certain fixed laws.

He then speaks of the mind, 'for its own gratification', using various figures of speech such as metonymy, abstraction, hyperbole, but actually there is little difference between imagination and fancy in his definitions. I have already given my interpretation of what are called figures of speech and will now give a definition of imagination as the faculty was exercised by Wordsworth himself. *It is the power by which we become so united,—or better, by which we realise our original unity with persons, things, situations, so completely,—that we perceive them by simple self-consciousness.* This definition closely approximates to Wordsworth's own definitions scattered throughout the Preface to *Lyrical Ballads*, in which he says, for example, of poetry,

> Its object is truth [   ] carried alive into the heart by passion: *truth which is its own testimony.*

The change from this definition to that of seventeen years afterwards, in the 1815 Edition, is the result of a change of attitude, to a state of mind which speaks of

> Ye Presences of Nature in the sky
> And on the earth! Ye Visions of the hills!
> And Souls of lonely places!
>> (*Prel. I*, 464)

> the great mass
> Lay bedded in a quickening soul.
>> (*Prel. III*, 134)

The very beginnings of this notion of presences and somethings and spirits Wordsworth notes in the First Book of *The Prelude*. At ten years old even, shades of the prison house of fear and discrimination had begun to close over the growing boy, for when he had done something wrong, he says,

> I heard among the solitary hills

> Low breathings coming after me, and sounds
> Of undistinguishable motion, steps
> Almost as silent as the turf they trod.
> > *(Prel. I,* 322)

Instead of realising that this feeling was due to the illusion of separation between himself and nature, the seeds of this fatal division between man and the outer world, and later, between God and Nature, were allowed to spring up, until in *Tintern Abbey* (1798) he utters the beautiful lines,

> And I have felt
> A presence that disturbs me with the joy
> Of elevated thoughts; a sense sublime
> Of something far more deeply interfused,
> Whose dwelling is the light of setting suns,
> And the round ocean and the living air,
> And the blue sky, and the mind of man:
> A motion and a spirit, that impels
> All thinking things, all objects of all thought,
> And rolls through all things.

The loftiness of the thought, the truth of the details, the eloquence of the whole, must not blind us to the fact that there is in this fruit the speck which, rotting inward, slowly mouldered all Wordsworth's poetry. What is wrong with pantheism? It is not that it is not true, it is rather that when expressed in words it becomes false; it is that our minds are somehow unfitted to receive it. When we say, 'All is God, this book is God, I am God', the very form of the thought, of the judgement, of the sentence, has in it

> the little rift within the lute,
> That by and by will make the music mute,
> And ever widening slowly silence all.

When we say 'This is God', in our minds, the part is divided from the whole. Becoming aware of this, we assert with dogged mysticism, 'The part is the whole', but in the very assertion of identity, the fatal separation is irrevocably there. Thus Wordsworth says, the breach widening,

> The immeasurable height
> Of woods decaying, never to be decayed,
> The stationary blasts of waterfalls,
> And in the narrow rent at every turn
> Winds thwarting winds, bewildered and forlorn,
> The torrents shooting from the clear blue sky,
> The rocks that muttered close upon our ears,

Black drizzling crags that spake by the way-side
As if a voice were in them, the sick sight
And giddy prospect of the raving stream,
The unfettered clouds and region of the Heavens,
Tumult and peace, the darkness and the light—
Were all like workings of one mind, the features
Of the same face, blossoms upon one tree;
Characters of the great Apocalypse,
The types and symbols of Eternity,
Of first, and last, and midst, and without end.

(Prel. VI, 624)

In 1800 Wordsworth had written,

Jehovah—with his thunder and the choir
Of shouting angels, and the empyreal thrones—
I pass them unalarmed,

(Recluse, 786)

a passage that is said to have upset Blake so much that he fell ill (the mystic out-mysticised for once!) but in the Fourth Book of *The Excursion* (about 1809 or after), Wordsworth makes full recantation:

One adequate support —
For the calamities of mortal life
Exists— one only; an assured belief
That the procession of our fate, howe'er
Sad or disturbed, is ordered by a *Being
Of infinite benevolence and power;*
Whose everlasting purposes embrace
All accidents, converting them to good.

Twenty years after, in 1842, this doctrine reached its logical and imbecile conclusion in one of the *Ecclesiastical Sonnets, Forms of Prayer at Sea,* where we are told that the crew, saved from shipwreck by God, are right to give solemn thanksgiving for His mercy (but how about those who were drowned, or died of thirst in an open boat?) and that English sailors will always win naval battles if they ask God to assist them.

Suppliants! the God to whom your cause ye trust
Will listen, and ye know that. He is just.

All this kind of thing comes from the intellectual separation of God and man and nature, a separation of man from Here and Now. Wordsworth says

Our destiny, our being's heart and home,
Is with infinitude, and only there.

(Prel. VI, 604)

It is not. Take no thought for the morrow, or for infinity or for eternity. Take no thought for what will happen five minutes afterwards, one minute afterwards. Blessed are the poor in spirit, now! Namu Amida Butsu, NOW!

7

POETRY IS EVERYDAY LIFE

(This Chapter, from 'Zen in English Literature and Oriental Classics', is preceded by one entitled 'Religion is Poetry'. Blyth does not force the syllogism, 'Therefore religion is everyday life, and everyday life religion', but this is strongly implied. See also the syllogism emboldened on page 85.)

From Aristotle down to Arnold it was considered that a great subject was necessary to the poet. Arnold says that the plot is everything. It is useless for the poet to

> imagine that he has everything in his own power; that he can make an intrinsically inferior action equally delightful with a more excellent one by his treatment of it.

Wordsworth stands outside this tradition by instinct and by choice. He chooses the aged, the poor, the idiot, the vagrant, but does not endeavour to make them 'delightful' at all. 'Nothing is inferior or superior, delightful or repugnant, but thinking makes it so'. What becomes, then, of the great subject? The answer is that on the one hand it is a concession to human weakness, which sees the house afire over the way as more thrilling than the flames of the sun, a toothache as more tragic than an earthquake or pestilence. On the other hand, the great subject is in its nature richer if only by mere quantity and mass. The fact that Lear is a King, Hamlet a Prince, Othello a General, and Caesar an Emperor, adds to the tragic force of the action, though intrinsically, to borrow Arnold's word, they are no more tragic than Jesus the Carpenter's son. Nevertheless, size is not meaningless. Even [Chuangtse], the arch-absolutist, points out that a cup cannot float in the quantity of water that will support a poppy seed.

But it is the poet, the man, who decides the meaning, the relation of quality to quantity. Thus Paul was converted by a supernatural light from Heaven and the voice of the ascended Christ; [Hsiang Yen], by the sound of a stone striking a bamboo.

To return to Wordsworth. Critics have often pointed out his inconsistency of practice and precept in regard to diction, but there are other contradictions more worthy of note. In the Preface to *Lyrical Ballads* he has the following notorious sentence:

> The principal object, then, proposed in these poems was to choose incidents and situations from common life, and to relate or describe

them, throughout, as far as was possible, in a selection of language really used by men, and, at the same time, *to throw over them a certain colouring of the imagination* whereby ordinary things should be presented to the mind in an unusual aspect; and further, and above all, *to make these incidents and situations interesting* by tracing in them, truly though not ostentatiously, the primary laws of our nature.

'To throw over them a certain colouring of the imagination'! This is a phrase that must have worked incalculable harm to English poetry during the next century and a half, though it is directly opposed to Wordsworth's actual practice. Look at the two following extracts and find if you can, 'the colouring of the imagination' which is thrown over them:

> No motion has she now, no force;
> She neither hears nor sees;
> Roll'd round in earth's diurnal course,
> With rocks, and stones, and trees.

These and the following are the greatest lines Wordsworth ever wrote:

> She died, and left to me
> This heath, this calm and quiet scene;
> The memory of what has been,
> And never more will be.

Wordsworth looks steadily at the object, and this is his greatness, as it is also Shakespeare's. Again, what an unfortunate phrase, 'to make these incidents and situations interesting'. It suggests a cook adding condiments, a little bit of alliteration here, a bit of onomatopoeia there, some personification, a paradox or two, and an unexpected, brilliant last line for the critics to quote. Wordsworth himself not only never does this (or almost never; the *Immortality Ode* is rather suspicious in places, and though successful, is still a *tour de force*) but himself says,

> O Reader! had you in your mind
> Such stores as silent thought can bring,
> O gentle Reader! you would find
> A tale in everything,

that is, poetry everywhere. Let us take *Michael* as an example.

In this poem of four hundred and eighty-two lines, there are five or six lines of what is ordinarily termed poetry, [   ] which might be overlooked, or rather, taken with the rest, by an earnest and careful reader. This so-called poem, then, is a piece of everyday country life, just as Dickens' novels are descriptions of everyday life and everyday city people. Two hard-working people had a son who was a failure and fled abroad. They died. This is not merely the whole story, there is no account of their despair and grief, not a word of it. Wordsworth avoids what would be called the chances which the story offers to wring the reader's feelings. Yet we feel the majesty, the dignity of man more than in Hamlet's most tragic speeches. Othello at his most poetic, Lear at his most pathetic, Macbeth at his most desperate, have not the grandeur of the old shepherd who

> still looked up to sun and cloud,
> And listened to the winds.

Why is this? It is because the true poetic life is the ordinary everyday life.

Of the Chinese poets Po Chü-i and T'ao Yüan-ming understood this fact best of all. Li Po, Tu Fu, and most of the lesser poets of the T'ang dynasty, as represented in the Tôshisen [anthology], are 'poetical' poets. The following is Po Chü-i:

> I take your poems in my hand and read them beside the candle;
> The poems are finished: the candle is low: dawn not yet come.
> With sore eyes by the guttering candle still I sit in the dark,
> Listening to waves that, driven by the wind, strike the prow of the boat.[1]

There is great art in the selection of facts presented, but no 'colouring of the imagination'; the incidents and situations are chosen 'from common life'. This is true also of the first of a series of thirteen poems by T'ao Yüan-ming, entitled *Reading the Book of the Seas and Mountains.*

> It is early summer: grass is rank, plants grow wildly,
> And the trees round my house are in full leaf.
> The birds rejoice in their nests here,
> And I too love my dwelling-place as dearly as they.
> I have ploughed my fields and sown them:
> Now at last, I have time to sit at home and read my books!
>
> The lanes are too narrow for fine carriages,
> And even my old friends are often turned back.
> Contentedly I pour out my wine,
> And partake of the lettuce grown in my own garden.

---

[1] *Waley's translation*

Borne on a soft eastern wind,
Light showers come.
Unrolling the Book of the Seas and Mountains,
I read the story of the King of Chou:
Gazing at sky and earth while yet we live—
How otherwise shall we take our pleasure here?[1]

In Li Po the subject and treatment is always romantic; the famous *Crows at Twilight* is typical:

Athwart the yellow clouds of sunset, seeking their nests
under the city wall,
The crows fly homeward. Caw! Caw! Caw! they cry
among the branches.
At her loom sits weaving silk brocade, one like the
Lady of Ch'inch'uan:
Their voices come to her through the window with its
curtains misty-blue.
She stays the shuttle; grieving, she thinks of her far-
distant lord:
In the lonely, empty room, her tears fall like rain.

Li Po had mystical leanings all his life, but especially in his youth and old age. In the poem *Answering a Question in the Mountains* he says,

I am asked why I live in the green mountains;
I smile but reply not, for my heart is at rest.
The flowing waters carry the image of the peach
blossoms far, far away:
There is an earth, there is a heaven, unknown to men.

Compare this with Obata's translation in *Li Po the Chinese Poet:*

Why do I live among the green mountains?
I laugh and answer not, my soul is serene:
It dwells in another heaven and earth belonging to no man.
The peach trees are in flower and the water flows on ....

[ ] When we come to Japanese poetry, which means Bashô, we find 'Poetry is everyday life' in its purest form. Bashô could and did write

---

[1]*See Waley for a different translation*

'poetical' poetry of the highest order. Scattered throughout this book will
be found a great number of this kind of poem; here are a few more:

> The sea darkens:
> Voices of the wild ducks
> Are dim and white.

> The autumn tempest!
> It blows along
> Even wild boars!

> The summer rains through the ages
> Have left undimmed then,
> The Hall of Gold.

> I heard the unblown flute
> In the deep summer shadows
> Of the Temple of Suma.

This remarkable poem with its similarity to Keats'

> Heard melodies are sweet, but those unheard
> Are sweeter: therefore, ye soft pipes, play on;
> Not to the sensual ear, but, more endear'd,
> Pipe to the spirit ditties of no tone

had a not dissimilar origin and background. Bashô visited Sumadera in the
summer and saw there the flute Atsumori used to play in the castle before his
death. In his heart he heard its thin melancholy notes. There is the same
thought in the following:

> *Kirishigure Fuji o minu hi zo omoshiroki*
> Veil'd from sight today
> In misty showers:
> Still, Mt. Fuji!

> *Ishiyama no i shi yori shiroshi aki no kaze*
> Whiter than the stones
> Of the Stony Mountain,
> The wind of autumn!

> *Koe ni mina nakishimaute ya semi no kara*
> The shell of a cicada:
> It sang itself
> Utterly away.

Samidare ni kakurenu mono ya Seta no hashi
The summer rains:
All things hidden
But the long bridge of Seta.

But where Bashô is at his greatest is where he seems most insignificant; the neck of a firefly, hailstones in the sun, the chirp of an insect, muddy melons, leeks, a dead leaf, — these are full of interest, meaning, value, that is, poetry, *but not as symbols of the Infinite, not as types of Eternity, but in themselves.* Their meaning is just as direct, as clear, as unmistakable, as complete and perfect, as devoid of reference to other things, as dipping the hand suddenly into boiling water. The mind is roused as with the sound of a trumpet. When you read one of the following it is just like opening a door and being confronted by a tiger. It is like suddenly seeing the joke of something. It is like being unexpectedly reprieved from the sentence of death.

Asagiri ni yogorete suzushi uri no tsuchi
The melons look cool,
Flecked with mud
From the morning dew.

Nebuka shiroku arai-tatetaru samusa kana
Just washed,
How chill
The white leeks!

Ishiyama no ishi ni tabashiru arare kana
The hail-stones
Glance off the rocks
Of the Stony Mountain.

Hiru mireba kubisuji akaki hotaru kana.
By day-light
The firefly has
A neck of red.

Matsutake ya shiranu ko no ha o hebari-tsuku
On the mushroom
Is stuck the leaf
Of some unknown tree.

Fuku tabi ni chô no inaoru yanagi kana
With every gust of wind,

> The butterfly changes its place
> On the willow.

Naturally, when the distinction between the poetical and unpoetical subject disappears (to attain this state is the true practical aim of a poet) foul is fair and fair is foul, to the pure all things are pure, nothing is unclean.

> *Tebana kamu oto sae ume no nioi kana*
> The sound of someone
> Blowing his nose with his hand;
> The scent of the plum flowers!

The sound of the nose-blowing, the scent of the flowers, which is more beautiful? The first may remind us of a long-lost, beloved friend; the second, of the death of a child who fell from the bough of a plum-tree. Beethoven may have got the motif of the first movement of the Fifth Symphony from some one's blowing his nose. Underneath all our prejudices for and against things, we must be free of them. This same freedom from the idea of dignity, that there are vessels of honour and vessels of dishonour, is shown in the following, full of life and truth:

> *Uguisu ya mochi ni fun suru en no saki*
> Look! the dried rice cakes
> At the end of the verandah—
> The *uguisu* is pooping on them !

More certainly than many things written in the Gospels, Christ went to the lavatory. This action was no less holy and no more symbolical than the breaking of bread and drinking wine at the Last Supper. Wherever bread is eaten, Christ's body is broken. Wherever wine is drunk, His blood is shed. But because of the hardness of our hearts we are taught to remember the Sabbath day to keep it holy, Easter, Pentecost, Christmas, Buddha's birthday, the Commemoration of Entering into Nirvana, the Day of His Enlightenment. These symbols are only crutches to our weakness, milk for babes. For,

> Every day is a good day,

as [Yün Men] said, every day is the best day, every moment is the best moment, and thus,

> Your everyday mind—that is the Way!

From morning to night, walking, eating, sleeping, praying, living, dying,

> Whatsoever thy hand findeth to do, do it with all thy might,

and again,

> Whether therefore ye eat or drink or whatsoever ye do, do it
> all to the glory of God.

One eye on the work, and one eye on God, one eye on the object,
the finite, and the other on the Infinite — this is not the meaning. 'With
all thy might' equals 'the glory of God', for as Blake says,

> Energy is Eternal Delight.

The distinction between ideal and real, man and God, individual and
universal, poetry and matter of fact, ordinary life and religion—it is this
illusory distinction that Zen seeks to break down. There is a saying attributed
to Christ:

> Render unto Caesar the things that are Caesar's and unto
> God the things that are God's.

This has a fine eloquence, but leaves the mind unillumined and uninspired.
The things of Caesar are the things of God. Sweeping a room, Caesar's room,
is sweeping God's room. There is a thrilling story told of Stevenson in this
connection. At Pitlochry, in 1881, when he saw a dog being ill-treated, he
at once interposed, and when the owner resented his interference and told
him, 'It's not your dog', he cried out, 'It's God's dog, and I'm here to protect
it!'

In English literature the best examples of the kind of poetry which takes
its material from the apparently trivial or disgusting, are Shakespeare's
songs; for example,

> When icicles hang by the wall,
> And Dick the shepherd blows his nail,
> And Tom bears logs into the hall,
> And milk comes frozen home in pail,
> When blood is nipp'd and ways be foul,
> Then nightly sings the staring owl,
> To-whit! To-who!— a merry note,
> While greasy Joan doth keel the pot.

When all aloud the wind doth blow,
And coughing drowns the parson's saw,
And birds sit brooding in the snow,
And Marian's nose looks red and raw,
When roasted crabs hiss in the bowl,
Then nightly sings the staring owl,
Tu-whit! Tu-who!— a merry note,
While greasy Joan doth keel the pot.

The last line, the refrain, is particularly noteworthy, because it is an epitome of 'natural' poetry, of the whole truth in art, where selection and arrangement is everything and the material indifferent, because all equally good and useful. Look at another example from *Martin Chuzzlewit:*

'I think, young woman,' said Mrs. Gamp to the assistant chamber maid, in a tone expressive of weakness, 'that I could pick a little bit of pickled salmon, with a nice little sprig of fennel, and a sprinkling of white pepper. I takes new bread, my dear, with jest a little pat of fresh butter, and a mossel of cheese. In case there should be such a thing as a cowcumber in the 'ous, will you be so kind as to bring it for I'm rather partial to 'em, and they does a world of good in a sick room. If they draws the Brighton Old Tipper here, I takes *that* ale at night, my love; it bein' considered wakeful by the doctors. And whatever you do, young woman, don't bring more than a shilling's-worth of gin and water-warm when I rings the bell a second time; for that is always my allowance, and I never takes a drop beyond!'

To explain the Zen, the religion, the poetry of this would be as difficult as to explain the humour of it: you either see it or not. Mrs. Gamp would be a match for any of the Ancient Worthies such as Rinzai, Ôbaku, or [Yün Men], because *she is herself,* she is true to herself and therefore not false to anything; she cannot be defeated by God, Nature, Circumstance, or their vice-regents, those who live by Zen. Mrs. Gamp is not divided from the pickled salmon or the bottle which she asks may be left

'on the chimley-piece, and let me put my lips to it when I am so dispoged',

as other people are by their notions of what is refined and vulgar, the distinction of material and spiritual. From this comes the gusto that is the hall-mark of Zen, of abundant life. Look at one more of Mrs. Gamp's speeches, flattering the undertaker's wife with eternal youth:

'There are some happy creeturs,' Mrs. Gamp observed, 'as time runs back'ards with, and you are one, Mrs. Mould: not that he need do nothing except use you in his most owldacious way for years to come, I'm sure; for young you are and will be. I says to Mrs Harris,' Mrs. Gamp continued, 'only t'other day; the last Monday evening fortnight as ever dawned upon this Piljian's Projiss of a mortal wale; I says to Mrs. Harris when she says to me, ' Years and our trials, Mrs. Gamp sets marks upon us all.' Say not the words Mrs. Harris if you and me is to be continual friends, for sech is not the case. Mrs. Mould,' I says, making so free, I will confess, as use the name' (she curtseyed here) ' is one of them that goes agen the obserwation straight; and never, Mrs. Harris, whilst I've a drop of breath to draw, will I set by, and not stand up, don't think it.'

Compare the words of this dirty, drunken, ghoulish, self-seeking, garrulous, greedy creature, with those of the refined, educated, idealistic poet W.B.Yeats:

> Though leaves are many the root is one;
> Through all the lying days of my youth
> I swayed my leaves and flowers in the sun;
> Now I may wither into the truth.

Which of the two has more life, more guts, more Zen? Whose view of old age and death is truer, those people who talk about

> Reality as a number of great eggs laid by the Phoenix and that these eggs turn inside out perpetually without breaking the shell,[1]

or those who like Mrs. Gamp and Falstaff and Gargantua, say with Dr. Johnson,

> I look upon it, that he who does not mind his belly will hardly mind anything else.

We eat hypocritically, wive in shame and stealth, talk of ideals, fritter our half-lives away. Mrs. Gamp shows us up, but we laugh to hide our feelings from ourselves; we laugh, as Byron said, that we may not weep. It is worth noting, by the way, that she comes into the story after about 400 pages; not as an afterthought, but, like life itself, when it happens. She grew as naturally out of Dickens' soul, as a yellow crocus comes out of the black earth in spring.

[1]*A Vision*, by W.B.Yeats

To return to Shakespeare. One of his songs,

> Full fathom five thy father lies,
> Of his bones are coral made;
> Those are pearls that were his eyes:
> Nothing of him that doth fade,
> But doth suffer a sea-change
> Into something rich and strange.
> Sea-nymphs hourly ring his knell:
> Ding-dong.
> Hark! now I hear them,—
> Ding, dong, bell.

is compared by Charles Lamb to a song of Webster's:

> Call for the robin redbreast and the wren,
> Since o'er shady groves they hover,
> And with leaves and flowers do cover
> The friendless bodies of unburied men;
> Call unto his funeral dole
> The ant, the field-mouse, and the mole
> To rear him hillocks that shall keep him warm
> And (when gay tombs are robb'd) sustain no harm;
> But keep the wolf far thence, that's foe to men,
> For with his nails he'll dig them up again.

Lamb says of them,

> As that is of the water, watery; so this is of the earth, earthy. Both have
> that intenseness of feeling which seems to resolve itself into the
> element it contemplates.

Shakespeare resolves himself into water, Webster into earth, Mrs. Gamp into
pickled salmon, Stevenson into a dog, Buddha into a flower, Gu-tei into his
own finger, Bashô into a frog.

But in this kind of thing there is a great danger again, of poetry losing
contact with facts, and as Mrs. Gamp herself states,

> Facts is stubborn things and can't be drove.

Poetry is not only ordinary life, it is common sense. Georgias Leontinus,
quoted by Aristotle, said,

Humour is the only test of gravity, and gravity of humour. For a subject which will not bear raillery is suspicious; and a jest which will not bear a serious examination is certainly false wit.

In the same way, poetry and common sense test each other.

> Here, with green Nature all around,
> While that fine bird the skylark sings,
> *Who now in such a passion is*
> *He flies by it and not his wings,*

says Davies, and this is true, and the fact is poetry.

Contrast Andrew Young's *March Hares*. This could never be countenanced by Zen, because not by common sense; it is not poetry, because it is false.

> I made myself as a tree
> No withered leaf twirling on me;
> No, not a bird that stirred my boughs,
> As looking out from wizard brows
> I watched those lithe and lovely forms
> That raised the leaves in storms.[1]

> I was content enough,
> Watching that serious game of love,
> That happy hunting in the wood,
> Where the pursuer was the more pursued,
> To stand in breathless hush
> With no more life myself than tree or bush.

If you make yourself as a tree, you can't watch hares. You live the life of a tree, dimly aware of day and night, the passage of the seasons. If you become a tree, you must become a tree and done with it. If you say the above verses mean, 'I watched the hares as a tree would watch them if it could do so', you are only talking like the natural philosopher who asked, 'How much wood could a woodchuck chuck, if a woodchuck could chuck wood?' If you are going to watch hares, you must forget yourself, whether you are 'content' or discontented, 'breathless' or otherwise. You must forget to compare yourself to a tree, and tell people your brows are 'wizard', whatever that means. You must become a hare and done with it, and the poem that comes out of that experience will be worth reading. This is just like M. Duthuit's Chinese recipe for painting bamboos:

[1] *second verse omitted*

Draw bamboos for ten years, become a bamboo, then forget all about bamboos when you are drawing.

When Bashô looked at an onion, he saw the onion; when he looked at the Milky Way, he portrayed the Milky Way; when he felt a deep unnameable emotion, he said so. But he did not mix them all up in a vague pantheistic stew or symbolic potpourri. In poetry, as in life itself, distinctness, the individual thing, directness is all-important.

Haiku does not [ ] aim at beauty. Like the music of Bach, it aims at significance, and some special kind of beauty is found hovering near. The real nature of each thing, and more so, of all things, is a poetical one. It is because Christ was a poet that men followed and still follow him, not Socrates. Socrates showed us our ignorance. Haiku shows us what we knew all the time, but did not know we knew; it shows us that we are poets in so far as we live at all. Here again is the connection between Zen and haiku, Zen which says,

Your ordinary mind,—that is the Way!

The essential simplicity of haiku and Zen must never be forgotten. The sun shines, snow falls, mountains rise and valleys sink, night deepens and pales into day, but it is only very seldom that we attend to such things.

Ezôshi ni shizu oku mise no haru no kaze
In the shop,
The paper-weights on the picture-books:
The spring wind!   Kitô

When we are grasping the inexpressible meaning of these things, this is life, this is living. To do this twenty-four hours a day is the Way of Haiku. It is having life more abundantly.

We may note in passing that Japanese readers will all have slightly different translations and meanings to give most of these verses. This is both the power and the weakness of haiku. It is a weakness in that we are not quite sure of the meaning of the writer. It is a power in that haiku demand the free poetic life of the reader in parallel with that of the poet. This 'freedom' is not that of wild irresponsibility and arbitrary interpretation, but that of the creation of a similar poetic experience to which the haiku points. It corresponds very much in English poetry to the different, the very different way in which people read the same poem.

(from the Preface to 'Haiku', Vol.1)

8

ZEN, ANIMISM, NATURE, LITERATURE

(This is the Introduction to 'History of Haiku', Vol.1)

8.1 Haiku and Zen

Haiku is an ascetic art, an artistic asceticism. Of the two elements, the ascetic is more rare, more difficult, of more value than the artistic. For this reason, Wordsworth remains the least understood of English poets, and has no disciples, or even imitators. Art is something that every woman is born with; every man begins to be a kind of artist when he falls in love. Asceticism is found, it is true, whenever a man gives up pleasure for pain, happiness for blessedness, when for example an athlete makes himself mentally and physically fit for a contest, but the asceticism spoken of here is not a means to an end. It is an end in itself, and therefore cannot be questioned; it cannot be explained or justified. It may seem odd that this sobriety of asceticism should be vitally connected with the piquancy of art. It should be noted however that art tends from life to artificiality, from the simple to the complex, the penny plain to the tuppence coloured, but **the art of haiku is as near to life and nature as possible, as far from literature and fine writing as may be, so that the asceticism is art and the art is ascetism.** This kind of thing we see in Chuangtse and Hanshan, Thoreau, Wordsworth, and Clare; and also in Bach, Giotto, Eckhart, Spinoza, Socrates, Cervantes, Conrad, and Stevenson; in Bashô and Issa. We cannot divide a certain kind of life from a certain kind of art, the truth from the beauty. Campion has a somewhat similar experience expressed in

> Great is Beauty's grace,
> Truth is yet as fair as she.

This asceticism is the antithesis of vulgarity, and yet there is nothing precious or affected or snobbish or highbrow about it.

The question of quantity and quality is a difficult one. The half is no doubt greater than the whole, but there is a limit to the less the better. Some senryu, or rather, pre-senryu, were of 14 syllables only, 7, 7. For example, from *Mutamagawa:*

> The one who loves more
> Slants the umbrella over the other.

Haiku is not a truncated or de-tailed waka[1]. It was the first stanza, so to speak,

---

[1] *see footnote on p.34*

of a very long poem, of perhaps 100 lines, and its potential independence was due to its being the first, and having a season word in it for subsequent stanzas. When however it was composed independently it still had the nature of 'a shock of mild surprise', a stab of enlightenment; the haiku poet

> Felt throughout this fleshly dress
> Bright shoots of everlastingness.

What Vaughan says here, in *The Retreat*, is worth considering a little in detail. 'Shoots' implies the shortness and strength of the experience, and this shortness corresponds to that of the form of haiku. 'Everlastingness' is poetry, and 'fleshly dress' points to the essentially physical, sensuous nature of the experience. Everlastingness is to some extent mental, but the experience is all in the body, and in all the body. **What distinguishes haiku from (other forms of) poetry is this physical, material, sensational character. and it might be termed what Buchanan called the pre-Raphaelites, 'the fleshly school of poetry', but with no sexual implications.** Actually, this absence of sex is a defect in haiku, overcompensated in senryu; it is the sexual element that gives to D. H. Lawrence's nature poetry its especially real and living character. The everlastingness and the fleshliness, unseparated and inseparable, unsymbolic and unsuggestive,—this is the characteristic of haiku. We find this kind of thing most of all in Thoreau, perhaps only in him.

Sometimes in haiku the material and the immaterial, the near and the far, the personal and the impersonal are brought together in too obvious a way:

> *Shiratsuyu ya imo no hatake no ama no gawa*
> White dew;
> Over the potato field,
> The Milky Way.   *Shiki*

> *Nowaki shite nezumi no wataru niwatazumi*
> The autumn storm
> Stopped blowing:
> A rat swam over the stream.   *Buson*

> *Take-en o donguri hashiru arashi kana*
> The storm
> Runs the chestnuts
> Over the bamboo verandah.   *Shiki*

[Elsewhere ,I have] asserted that haiku is an aspect of Zen; that haiku is Zen, Zen directed to certain selected natural phenomena. The choice of subjects is significant, reflecting as it does the character of the haiku poets, their nationality, social position, and world-view. Those things omitted (war, sex, poisonous plants and ferocious animals, floods, pestilences, earthquakes and so on) are all dangerous and menacing to human life. We wish to forget them, and must do so if we are to live our short life in any sort of mental ease.

An old battlefield, wild boars, things shaking in an earthquake, typhoons as merely strong winds,—such things are occasionally treated, but there is nothing of Hemingway about the haiku poets. Zen includes, haiku excludes; here is a great difference between the two. Zen is yea-saying, haiku also, but there is also the nay-saying of an art that avoids ugliness and hate and untruth, that abhors the sentimentality and romance and vulgarity which Zen will view with equanimity.

What is Zen? The following, by Bernard Phillips, is one of the best explanations I have come across so far. It concerns 'Zen practice', but this term is a sort of tautology, for Zen is practice; without practice there is no Zen.

> Zen literature abounds in admonitions against seeking Buddhahood by any sort of contrivance. What, then, can it mean to 'practise Zen'? Are not *zazen, koan* study, sutra chanting, etc., all 'contrivances'? On the other hand, if all such are to be eliminated, how will the Zen student ever progress from his initially unenlightened condition to a state of enlightenment?

> Zen practice is at bottom the act of giving oneself, of entering wholly into one's actions. As this giving becomes more and more complete, one's practice and one's life both attain to an ever-deeper degree of integrity and reality. It is not sufficient simply to practise a formal routine. One must enter into the practice and become one with it, so that it is no longer an action performed by a doer who is external to the action. What is decisive is just this *entering in* and not the formal niceties of the practice in and of themselves. To the degree that the doer is divorced from the deed, to that extent is the deed a mere formality, an act of the ego and lacking in the ring of truth. To give up the ego is just to abandon the position of exteriority to one's actions and to be 'all there' in them.

> Zen practice is thus not a set of operations designed to achieve an external goal. In Zen, the effort and the result are not two different things, the means and the goal are not to be separated, the finding occurs in the very seeking itself. For ultimately, what is sought is the wholeness of the seeker, and this emerges only in the wholeheartedness of the seeking. Whatever specific form the practice may take, it is not the form *per se* which is efficacious, for that is only a mould into which the seeker endeavours to pour himself.

Zen itself is beyond the dichotomy of form and no-form, of contrivance and no-contrivance, of 'square' and 'beat'. A no-contrivance which opposes itself to contrivance is only another kind of contrivance. That is truly uncontrived which stems from the Buddha Heart, that is, from the ego-less union with life. The real task is to achieve this union with life, for only in this way is life transformed from a formality to a reality. This union with life is not accomplished by a revolt against forms, but by an entry into one's actions.

How is this entry into life to be achieved? The only word of advice is: Do not seek to find out what to do. Every *what to do* is only a general recipe, that is, an abstraction. You will never come into the truth of your own being riding on the back of an abstraction. If you know *what to do*, be sure it is the wrong thing.

If, as a corollary of this, we take Zen to be the essence of all art literature, music, and worth-activity, we must be able to see at the back of, for example, English poetry and haiku, some form or other of this 'entering into the activity'. For all the irreconcilable and fundamental differences between the two, they must have the equally fundamental quality of being (the result of) unification, the re-unification of two separate modes of being. In Zen, the doer and the deed are undivided and undividable (though at the same time they are divided and divisible). What corresponds to this unity in English verse, and in haiku?

The essence of English literature, that is, poetry in verse or prose, is that the sound-rhythm-intonation meaning and the intellectual meaning of the (spoken) words are one. From this arises the fact that a poem is not capable of an explanation, which is at best an analysis of the symbolic meaning of the sounds etc., a paraphrase of the thought, and a fusion of the two (really four). English poetry is thus a kind of onomatopoeia, not of the cheap, calculated, Tennysonian variety, where the sound of the word is the sound of the thing, but in which the word is the thing and the thing is the word, spontaneously, naturally, 'accidentally'.

The theory of the matter is that a thing is not really a thing until it has a word, a spoken word, as its own expression; and a word is not really a word, that is, is not a poetic word, unless it is part of a thing, the extension of it, the thing heard, the thing speaking. Things without words, and words in a dictionary, have no existence. They are either dead or not yet born. A (real) word does not express a thing. No thing can express another. A (real) thing is a thought-thing, a thing thinking, a thing wording. 'I see men as trees walking'. Trees are men that can't walk. Thoreau says, 'The words of some men are thrown forcibly against you.' These words are the men themselves. Thus the 100% entering of the doer into his deed, in Zen, corresponds to the interpenetrability of word and thing in English poetry. 'The flesh is made word, and dwells among us'. [   ]

In haiku, the two entirely different things that are joined in sameness are poetry and sensation, spirit and matter, the Creator and the Created. The coldness of a cold day, the heat of a hot day, the smoothness of a stone, the whiteness of a seagull, the distance of the far-off mountains, the smallness of a small flower, the dampness of the rainy season, the quivering of the hairs of a caterpillar in the breeze— these things, without any thought or emotion or beauty or desire, are haiku.

Zen and (European) poetry and haiku and senryu have all a sameness, in that two opposite things, or things of different categories are united in one. They all have a difference, in that it is different things that are united. The schema is this:

Zen   : Doer is deed
Poetry   : Word is thing
Haiku   : Meaning is sensation
Senryu   : Enlightenment is illusion

In the beginning was the Actor, not the Act, as Goethe mistakenly says; the Word. To avoid materialism, we may say that the action is an extension of the actor, the thing is an extension of the word, *mayoi* of *satori*, sensation of meaning. But they are all hens and eggs really. One does not come before the other in time, or in essence, or in value. But yet the actor and the act, the thing and the word, enlightenment and illusion, meaning and sensation, are all two things, not one. The hen is not an egg; the egg is not a hen.

8.2 Animism

The essence of all nature poetry is animism (more exactly, animatism), the experience that each thing is 'alive', not merely animate or inanimate. Indeed God is The Great Animist, or Animiser, 'for unto Him all live'. Animism is thus the essence of divinity and therefore of humanity. Further, we are most human when we realise that not only stones and trees and gods are alive, but even human beings are. The highest point a man can reach is to know that he himself is not merely alive, but 'alive'. What is meant by 'alive'? It means having a direction, a purpose, a will. Things want. Things love, as Shelley tells us, following and transcending Plato and Dante. There is also the animism of place of D. H. Lawrence, the 'spots of time' of Wordsworth, and the inveterate tendency of the human mind to personify the very abstractions they have separated from human beings possessing these qualities.

Animism is of course at its best when silent. When explicit,

> And 'tis my faith that every flower
> Enjoys the air it breathes,
> *(Wordsworth: Lines written in Early Spring)*

it is a rational expression of something poetical. It is not poetry, it is not the thing living and talking, but only one thing chattering about another. By primitive man and a child ('thou best philosopher') animism is taken for granted. It cannot be despised in them as a superstition, for it is not something taught or learnt. On the contrary, as Wordsworth tells us in the *Immortality Ode*, this 'aliveness' of all things becomes overlaid by and confused with the aliveness and unaliveness taught and learned later. The function of the intellect is to distinguish between unalive and alive, but it has an additional and more important work, to mark the difference between 'alive' and alive. 'Alive' is absolute; it has no contrary, other than the non-perception of this aliveness which simply means that it is only the living who can know what 'living' is, for 'the dead know not anything'. What is lost by education (and how much this is Thoreau tried to teach us) must somehow be regained. The intellect perceives the loss, and points to the cause and prescribes the remedy. Christ and Plotinus and Eckhart; Traherne, Vaughan, Blake, Wordsworth, Clare, and D. H. Lawrence; and more indirectly Homer and Cervantes, Bach and Mozart, help us to return to Nature, that is, to our own nature, which is, as the most living thing in a living universe, to live in its life.

The animism of haiku is hardly ever explicit. There is little personification. But the Shinto belief that the sea is 'a mighty Being', that the mountain is a god, is not far from Vaughan's stones that are 'deep in contemplation'. Unlike the stones of Jerusalem, however, they would never go so far as to 'cry out'. So with Bashô's animism, as when Homer says the sun rises or the moon sets, 'we can hardly detect the enthusiasm of the bard'.

Japanese literature as a whole, and haiku in particular, has no mysticism in it. In Japan, the Buddhist doctrine of reincarnation confirmed the intuitions of the early Japanese. Animals and plants and senseless things were not merely 'senseful' but our poor relations, even, it may be, our own father or mother. Taoism was animistic to a superstitious (shamanistic) degree. Confucianism, a yet stronger influence in Japan, as providing something lacking in the Japanese character, loved ritual rather than living creatures, and affected only the already unsavably unpoetical people.

The Japanese, not in any case a nation of philosophers, never thought over the question of 'the pathetic fallacy'. Even nowadays, the dilemma is too intellectual, that is, too remote from ordinary, animal existence, to arouse interest. Is the foam cruel and crawling, as Kingsley said, or pretended that it was, and as Ruskin said it was not? Or, a different problem, was it Kingsley's mind that was cruel and crawling, and the foam just air bubbles? The answer is that the sea is alive; it loves and hates; it moans, it has many voices. But these words are not dictionary words, and the sea is not kind sometimes and cruel sometimes. It is never kind, and never cruel. But it is always 'kind', always 'cruel', always 'kind-cruel'. Wordsworth speaks of the 'unutterable love' of ocean and earth. 'Unutterable' does not mean 'which cannot be uttered'. It signifies that this love is the real thing that even we feel sometimes, in the midst of our loving and hating, attraction and repulsion.

When Japanese, that is to say, poetical Japanese (decreasing in number and also in Japaneseness) read a haiku, their standard of judgement, by a combination of heredity and environment, is as follows. **Positively, the haiku must express a new or newly perceived sensation, a sudden awareness of the meaning of some common human experience of nature or man. Negatively, and more importantly, it must, above all things, not be explanatory, or contain a cause and its effect.** Even in the case of Bashō's all-too-famous *Furu-ike ya*, the sound of the water is not a consequence of the presence of a pond, and the jumping in of a frog; these are not even antecedent circumstances. The old pond is there; it exists in its own right and has intrinsic value, as we see by the particle *ya*. The jumping in of the frog is grammatically adjectival, so that the sound of the water is not consequent, either in reason or in time, upon the jumping in of the frog. Both are coexistent, that is, coeternal. The old pond continues in time; the jumping in and the sound of the water are timeless. Or we may say, conversely, that the silence of the old pond continues timelessly, whereas the sound of the water is as a bubble upon that river of silence. This mystical and also mystifying atmosphere is due to the absence of thought, the transcendence of cause and effect, but a Japanese reader of haiku is far from aware of all this. He simply rejects intellectual components as 'not haiku' instinctively. Moral elements are also rejected as being generalities. Thus haiku has nothing to do with the Good, the True, or the Beautiful. There is nothing good, true, or beautiful about the sound of the water of the pond which this frog jumps into.

An English reader (poetical, and decreasing also in numbers and quality) of English nature poetry appreciates the richness of the verse, its overtones, the meaning-sound of the words, the physico-spiritual dancing, the heightening of his sensitivity to the significance of the whole and its parts, and of their interrelation. The more beauty the better. Morality, if subsumed into the topic and unseparated from it, as it is not in

> He prayeth best, who loveth best
> All things both great and small,
> *(Coleridge: Ancient Mariner)*

is an enrichment of the verse. Intellectuality, in the same way, something for the mind to meditate on, is an additional attraction. **Haiku is in danger of excessive purity. Devoid of beauty, intellectuality, and emotion, it may easily fall into triviality.** English poetry may wallow, in a Wagnerian manner, in a mass of emotion and words, with Keats and Hopkins, or involve itself in abstraction and ethics, as in Shelley and Browning. To say that the best parts of English nature poetry are those most like haiku would be too cruel, too provoking, perhaps even untrue, but the reverse is not a fact. **Haiku is at its best when it is simply Wordsworthian, that is, Wordsworth at his most simple, 'a sort of thought in sense'. It is at this point that haiku and English nature poetry coincide.**

Last of all, **it is necessary to state with some vehemence that haiku is not symbolic, that is, not a portrayal of natural phenomena with some meaning behind them.** In *Haiku and Haikai,* published by the Nippon Gakujutsu Shinkôkai in 1958, and in which the present author is said to be one of the (minor) collaborators, it asserts that 'most contemporary haiku poets believe that haiku is symbolistic, that is, it seeks to represent ideas and emotions by indirect suggestion, and to attach a symbolic meaning to particular objects.' It is then stated that Bashô held this theory, and the following quotations are given as evidence, from the *Sanzôshi, Zoku Goron,* and *Yamanaka Mondô* respectively: —

> When our master told us to learn about the pine-tree from the pine-tree and about the bamboo from the bamboo, he meant that we should transcend self and learn.....To learn means to submerge oneself into the object until its intrinsic nature becomes apparent, stimulating poetic impulse.
> Every form of insentient existence—plants, stones, or utensils— has its individual feelings similar to those of men.
> Make the universe your companion, always bearing in mind the true nature of all creation—mountains and rivers, trees and grasses, and humanity—and enjoy the falling blossoms and scattering leaves.

Bashô is declaring his belief in animism, the origin and basis of all religion and poetry. He is saying that each thing is, not has, infinite value. There is no separation between the thing and its meaning, no finding 'the universal in particular natural objects or human beings', not 'an awareness of something infinite and eternal of which they are the symbols'. One thing is not used to imply another thing. A single paulownia leaf falling is not a symbol of autumn, any more than the gleaner and the winnower, the reaper and the wine-presser are symbols in the *Ode to Autumn*. These people are autumn. No autumn, no falling leaf; no falling leaf, no autumn. And to the poet they are not parts of the season; each thing is the whole season.

8.3 Nature in Japanese Literature

A view of nature which is not utilitarian or scientific, in other words which is not nothing at all, is a poetical view of some kind. Literature itself, which is poetry in verse or prose, is a view of nature, the nature which is in man no less, and no more, than it is in the outer world. In *A Week on the Concord* Thoreau says that literature must be as natural as nature itself:

> As naturally as the oak bears an acorn, and the vine a gourd, a man bears a poem, either spoken or done.

Thus the above title should be: Nature *is* Japanese Literature.

Omitting the climate, topography, and all the other physical environmental factors, very important no doubt, but somehow not very interesting, and therefore not very important, we may say that the Japanese view and the English view of nature were the result of the innate character of the two races, and the influence of other cultures upon it. In the case of Japan, the influences are two, Indian, and Chinese; Korea influenced Japan greatly in sculpture and pottery. It should be noted in passing that the Indian, Korean, and Chinese cultures were already to a great extent blended when they reached Japan.

The aboriginal Chinese view of nature was no doubt like that of the Japanese and the English and the Indian,—an instinctive animism, but in China this feeling that all things are equally alive developed not only into shamanism, as elsewhere, but into the Taoism of Laotse and Chuangtse, in which all nature palpitates with life, and yet has philosophical implications for the thoughtful mind. With them, Taoism became a lofty yet homely mysticism, the object of life being a re-union of microcosmic man with the macrocosmos. How? Laotse answers, with Wordsworth, 'Let nature be your teacher!'

Confucianism, on the whole anti-poetical, appealed to anti-poetical Japanese. Confucius loved music, and poetry perhaps, and believed no doubt that his principles of conduct for man were 'natural', but he seems to have had little interest in Nature for its own sake. In the *Analects* it is written,

> Standing by a stream, Confucius said, 'Never ceasing, it flows
> on and on like this!'

but this kind of poetry was appreciated by the Zen poets of Japan.

The Buddhism which went to China was late Buddhism mingled with a Hinduism that was both pre-Buddhistic and post-Buddhistic. Primitive Buddhism was apparently a pedantic, moral, repetitious, unpoetical, non-religious affair, and could have had no effect upon the Chinese or Japanese people worth affecting. Hinduism was a different matter. Its all-soul-ism, contrasted with the no-soul-ism of early Buddhism, fitted in perfectly with the vague pantheism and explicit animism of primitive Shinto. Actually, as we see in the *Upanishads*, the Indian hermits of a millenium before Christ went beyond the animism of primitive man, by which man is a body-spirit among other, and all other, body-spirits, to a realisation that each man is himself The Body Spirit. 'You are It'. What Laotse and Chuangtse had found out by thinking, the ancient Indians discovered by practice. It was two thousand years before the Chinese Zen monks did the same thing again, in their own way.

Late Buddhism, with its doctrine of the Void, which has a remarkable correspondence in existentialism, made man not Everything, as in Hinduism, but Nothing, not the negative nothing of primitive Buddhism, but something positive, from which all things exfoliate. In this Nothing, all things are equal, because infinite. In this Silence, all things speak. We are not superior to nature, nor yet inferior to 'it', but of one substance with it.

The most direct influence upon Japanese and the Japanese view of nature was of course Chinese poetry, though Chinese painting must also have had a great effect. The prevailing tone of Chinese poetry is that of a melancholy subjectivism; there is no Wordsworthian joy. The Chinese poet sees himself in nature, or sees nature separated from himself, but himself is always there. Coleridge says in *Dejection*, 'Lady, we receive but what we give', and this is true of all but the deepest poetry. In the *Manyôshû*, allusions to nature are very frequent in the *chôka*, longer poems, but it is not easy to find a whole tanka (waka) devoted to nature only. The following is an example, by Ôtomo no Yakamochi, composed about 750 A.D.

> The cuckoo calls
> Among the leafy tree-tops
> Of the summer mountain,
> Far, far-off
> His echoing voice.

In a *chôka* by the same poet, written in 747 A.D., we see the animism (animatism) of the Japanese of Manyô times. Speaking of Mount Futagami, in Toyama Prefecture, the poet says:

> Is it because it is a god it is so sublime?
> Is it because it is a mountain it is so delightful to see?

Bashô read such verses in the *Manyôshû*; he read the Chinese poets, the greatest of them all perhaps, T'ao Yüan-ming, who ends one of the most famous of his poems with the lines:

> In these things (of Nature) there is a deep meaning,
> But when we try to express it, we forget the words.

Could Bashô remember the words which T'ao Yüan-ming forgot? Could he write something which should be beyond words, or, better still, *before* words? The answer is the following:

> *Hiyahiya to kabe o fumaete hirune kana*
> A noon-day nap;
> Pressing the feet on the wall,
> How cool!

This may seem an anti-climax; indeed, it is. It is coming back to earth (the wall is made of earth) with a thud, but it is also doing what Wordsworth did, looking at the rocks, the valleys, the mountains, only looking,

> nor any interest
> Unborrowed from the eye.
> *(Tintern Abbey, l.82)*

Bashô's verse has no interest unborrowed from the soles of his feet. It is the poetry of 'pure' sensation. More than a hundred years after Bashô, Crabbe has *his* anti-climax to the beauties of *L'Allegro* and *Il Penseroso*:

> Here on its wiry stem, in rigid bloom,
> Grows the salt lavender that lacks perfume.
> Here the dwarf sallows creep, the sept-foil harsh,
> And the soft slimy mallow of the marsh.

Wiry, rigid, salt, lacks, dwarf, creep, harsh, soft, slimy— with these words Crabbe teaches us something never taught before. Just as Bashô has no emotion, and Wordsworth no thought, Crabbe has no beauty; all three have only poetry, only nature.

74

8.4 The English View of Nature

The 'original' English view of nature has been affected by Christianity, and by Greek, Latin, French, and Italian cultures. The Anglo-Saxons, as far as the monkish transcribers inform us, seem to have been quite different from the Manyô Japanese. The poetry, the nature they wanted and willed and chose was that of danger, winter, solitude, of a bareness and bleakness that comes out again, after a thousand years of Mediterranean allurement to flowers and sunny skies, in the early Wordsworth, and Hardy always:

> the dark waves,
> The sea-birds bathing, spreading their wings,
> Rime and snow falling, mingled with hail.

Buddhism deepened and saddened the life-loving Japanese of the 6th century. Christianity had a sentimentalising and deadening effect upon the English view of nature. According to orthodox Christianity, the enemies of God and man are 'the world, the flesh, and the devil'. Nature belongs to the first two, and perhaps also to the third. God is infinitely above us; animals are infinitely below us. The Japanese view is still that of the author of *Beowulf.* Grendel is part demon, part man, part bear, or rather, not part, but one thing with three aspects; three things with one name. By the time we get to Milton, animals have no connection even with one another:

> Much less can bird with beast, or fish with fowl,
> So well converse, nor with the ox the ape.

These lines are quoted with disapproval by White of Selborne. Having no souls, animals have no value or meaning or poetry. Often useful, sometimes ornamental, always dangerous, nature is something to escape from. The Mediterranean cultures were all man-loving, nature-hating. To come across lines in Greek and Roman literature which show a poetical understanding of nature is a rare thing, and all the more a happy one. In *A Week on the Concord* Thoreau quotes the following from Virgil:

> Now the buds swell on the joyful stem...

> The apples lie scattered everywhere, each under its tree.

The first of these, in its animism, is reminiscent of Keats' 'Oh, happy, happy boughs!' and the second of a haiku by Buson:

> White dew on the bramble,
> One drop
> On each thorn.

75

Though the effect of the view of nature (if such it may be called) of the Mediterranean nations on that of the English was pernicious, with the notable exception of Hebrew (religious) literature, it may be said that by reaction it helped to produce the mysticism of Herbert, Vaughan, Traherne, Blake, Wordsworth, and Shelley. The *Auguries of Innocence* says:

> He who the ox to wrath has mov'd
> Shall never be by woman lov'd.
> The wanton boy that kills the fly
> Shall feel the spider's enmity.

The first two lines state that women (really) love only men that (really) love living creatures. This is true in my experience. The second two lines are less moral and psychological, and more mystical. The cruel man suffers the fate of the spider; the sin *is* the punishment.

The truly religious attitude to nature, which is the religious attitude *of* nature, is seen in the following line of Vaughan:

> For stones are deep in admiration.

Very different, and yet the same, is Bashô's verse written in spring at Nikkô:

> *Aratô to aoba wakaba no hi no hikari*
> Ah, how glorious
> The young leaves, the green leaves,
> Glittering in the sunshine!

The leaves share in Bashô's admiration.

Thoreau's attitude is always religious; on the death of his dearly beloved brother John:

> Soon the ice will melt, and the blackbirds sing along the river which he frequented, as pleasantly as ever. The same everlasting serenity will appear in this face of God, and we will not be sorrowful, if he is not.

This has the same meaning, the same tone as the conclusion of *The Matthew Passion*, which is Bach's view of Nature.

The moral attitude to nature is especially English; we cannot find anything in Japanese literature like Tennyson's 'nature red in tooth and claw', or

Arnold's *Morality*. Or we may say that the morality of nature is taken so much for granted by the Japanese that it is completely implicit, 'for Nature cannot err'. The intellectual, which means the scientific or philosophical aspect of nature, is also absent from Japanese literature. There is no Gilbert White, Darwin, Bates, or Hudson in Japan.

The aesthetic attitude, the idea that Beauty is truth, truth Beauty, was largely that of the Japanese poets up to the second half of the 17th century. In English literature, however, in Anglo-Saxon poetry, *Piers Plowman*, Chaucer, Skelton, the metaphysical poets, Swift, Burns and so on, ugliness was seen as more meaningful than beauty, but it has never been really firmly grasped and explicitly stated that ugliness is closer to poetry than beauty, just as the sinner is more religious than the good people Christ did not die to save. This paradoxical fact the Japanese people discovered-created in senryu, where the weakness and folly and hypocrisy of mankind are seen as more interesting, that is, more poetical, that is, more human than its greatest virtues. However, haiku are often as devoid of beauty as the lines quoted before of Crabbe. An example is the following by Shiki:

> *Amagaya ni hizakana no niou atsusa kana*
> In the fisherman's hut
> The smell of dried fish,—
> Ah, the heat!

The unique contribution of Japan to world culture was their poetry of sensation; we find it everywhere in English poetry, but not in isolation. An example from Wordsworth;

> Or the swan stirs the reeds, his neck and bill
> Wetting, that drip upon the water still.

The beauty of the swan, or the lake, is not the point here.

The emotional attitude to nature is found in waka, but not, strictly speaking, in haiku. Emotion is certainly a value (love, by the way, is not an emotion; it is another name for the religious value). Coldness of heart is as inhuman as lack of brains. As Kierkegaard said, 'It is impossible to exist without passion', but haiku seems to omit it, or rather, digests it completely into the sensation.

Humour is latent in every good haiku; its lack in Milton is perhaps only apparent. Underneath all the majesty there is some sort of pretence. We know it is really all a play, a comedy. It is not our world, whole and complete, but only a part of it. Man is the spectator and the actor in this drama, but, as

Emerson says, Nature bites her lips as she watches the antics of her puppets. Sometimes, but this is rare, the doll glances back at the puppeteer, and they wink at each other.

The animistic value is the most important of all. It is for lack of this that the world is dying, almost dead. An interesting, well-known example of animism from *In Memoriam:*

> Thy voice is on the rolling air;
> I hear thee where the waters run;
> Thou standest in the rising sun,
> And in the setting thou art fair.

A dead man is alive, as alive as the lifeless sun. We may compare this to a remarkable verse by Bashô, also on the death of someone he knew:

> *Tsuka mo ugoke waga naku koe wa aki no kaze*
> Shake, O tomb!
> My weeping voice
> Is the wind of autumn.

English nature poetry comes to exist when nature speaks with the voice of the poet; when the meaning of the words is the sound of the words, and the sound is the meaning. This is a sublime onomatopoeia, and it is to be heard also in haiku. However, English (nature) poetry is strongly physical; one may call it sexual. Examples from Keats, with true onomatopoeia:

> Fast-fading violets cover'd up in leaves...

> And full grown lambs loud bleat from hilly bourn...

Waka [tanka] also are such beautiful things in beautiful words which are the things speaking, but haiku are ordinary things in ordinary words. Further, haiku is both more physical and more spiritual than the lines of Keats quoted above. More physical in that it goes back to the sensation; more spiritual in eschewing beauty and morality and thought. Or shall we say that they are so latent as to be hidden from the intellectual eye. To be compared and contrasted with Keats' lines, a verse by Buson:

> *Jiguruma no todoro to hibiku botan kana*
> The heavy wagon
> Rumbles by;
> The peony quivers.

In haiku the words are less important than the sensation—of size, of heaviness, of strength, and of weakness—that gave birth to them, that hardly existed however as a cause until the effect arose. From the expression we go back to the impression, and, as T'ao Yüan-ming said, forget (the words of) the expression.

John Clare is the greatest English *nature* poet, just as Wordsworth is the greatest English nature *poet*, but he struggles in vain against the words of the grammar book, of the publisher, of English literature, which smother him as completely as Desdemona was smothered by Othello's passion. But perhaps it is after all a good thing. At the end of a poem, *Insects*, Clare says that they

> Are fairy folk in splendid masquerade
> Disguised, as if of mortal folk afraid,
> Keeping their merry pranks a mystery still,
> Lest glaring day should do their secrets ill.

8.5 Haiku in English Literature

Haiku being the poetry of sensation, ideally speaking what happens is this. We receive, or create, a sensation, a mere sensation, almost entirely physical and mechanical. It then becomes humanised, and at this stage is called in Zen, *dai-ichi nen*. To this are added emotions, and then thoughts, and more emotions and more thoughts, so that we get *dai-ni nen*. Haiku is *dai-ichi nen*, but is not mere description, just photography. One of the worst things in the world is mere sensation smeared all over with emotion and thought, as in *The Family of Man*. An example of this in English poetry is Tennyson's famous line:

> The moan of doves in immemorial elms.

The same sort of thing in an equally famous haiku:

> *Natsukusa ya tsuwamono-domo ga yume no ato*
> The summer grasses,
> All that remains,
> Of the warriors' dreams.

On the other hand, Japanese haiku is sometimes weak because, though it does not add human emotion to poetical sensation, it does not add the human will to the will of nature.

The poet may speak of himself, if it is in the same 'sensational' way. Wordsworth does so in the following:

> I wandered, lonely as a cloud,
> That floats on high o'er vales and hills.

This is haiku because the poet sees himself as a cloud, a kind of *unsui* [a mendicant monk]; sees that he is a cloud, until all at once he sees something else,

> a crowd,
> A host of golden daffodils;
> Beside the lake, beneath the trees,
> Fluttering and dancing in the breeze.

Then the third haiku comes much later, after he has returned home, after he has done no work, and when he is lying idly on his couch:

> And then my heart with pleasure fills,
> And dances with the daffodils.

The sensation of floating in the sky, the sensation of the 'jocund' dancing of the daffodils, and the sensation of his own dancing with 'pleasure' together with the daffodils,—these are all tending to emotion, but somehow avoid it. Poetic joy is not an emotion, any more than real love is, and this we see in other lines of Wordsworth:

> The one blasted tree,
> And the bleak music from that old stone wall.

Haiku avoids the two most interesting parts of human life, war and sex. For this reason, Burns' best lines are not haiku (he is full of senryu[1]):

> My Mary's asleep by thy murmuring stream,
> Flow gently! sweet Afton, disturb not her dream.

Burns here expresses his genuine feeling, his thoughts as he watches woman in the arms of nature. Mary is at her most beautiful, Burns at his most moral; it is a kind of religion of sex. But what the haiku poets discovered, though it was never put into words explicitly, was that poetry is not thought, is not emotion, is not beauty, is not morality, is not religion, but something else. And if thought and emotion and beauty and so on are considered by someone as desirable, then we may say to such a person,' Seek ye first the kingdom of poetry, and all these things shall be added unto you'.

Haiku has so far been taken to be equivalent to poetry, but what is the difference between haiku-like English poetry and un-haiku-like poetry? What

---

[1] *If you are not familiar with the distinction between haiku and senryu, you may like to refer to section 13.*

is the common element, if any, in the poetry of Homer and Kâlida'sa and Bashô? Is there such a thing as POETRY, something which

fills, and bounds, connects, and equals all?

As suggested above, haiku is the poetry of meaningful touch, taste, sound, sight, and smell; it is humanised nature, naturalised humanity, and as such may be called poetry in its essence. Sappho's famous verse,

Evening Star, that bringest back all that lightsome Dawn hath scattered afar, thou bringest the sheep, thou bringest the goat, thou bringest the child home to the mother...

is not haiku, because of the personification of the star; the pathos of the child, who does not know what takes him home; the grandeur of the conception. In haiku the child is seen as a child, the star as a star. There is no attempt to bring them together, at least in a serious way. Man has no dignity, nature no majesty. A small, nameless hill is better than Mount Fuji, best of all when 'half-hidden from the eye'. Haiku is the counterpart in literature of, 'He who would be master of all, let him be a servant'.

It may be asked, how can we distinguish between mere objectivity and poetry, if thought and emotion are in both cases omitted? The answer is that we feel it in the choice of words. An example from Crabbe,

Hardy and high, above the slender sheaf,
The slimy mallow waves her silken leaf.

The harvest of corn is thin, and half-withered, but the weeds, like the soft hairy mallow, grow triumphantly in this sandy soil. The alliteration and the onomatopoeia (on l and m, in the second line) are also remarkable. We see the same in the following, also by Crabbe:

Beneath an ancient bridge, the straiten'd flood
Rolls through its sloping banks of slimy mud.
(The Lover's Journey, l.109)

It might also be asked, how about waka [tanka] in English literature? The difference between waka and haiku is not merely that of length, at least of physical length. Waka is spiritually more expansive, and aims at beauty rather than poetry. So Milton's *L'Allegro* and *Il Penseroso* are close to waka, or rather renga, though sometimes to haiku as well:

Oft on a Plat of rising ground,
I hear the far-off Curfeu sound

Over som wide-water'd shoar
Swinging slow with sullen roar.

In the history of English literature we find the haiku spirit everywhere but often mixed with other elements more or less consciously omitted by the Japanese haiku poets. In *Beowulf* we have lines such as:

Thence the welter of waters washes up
Wan to welkin when winds bestir
Evil storms, and air grows dusk,
And the heavens weep.

This is the drearier aspect of nature beloved of the haiku poets, but there is a lack of sobriety, a dramatic element caused by and the cause of the alliterative form, that makes it, from the haiku point of view, a little false. It lacks 'the modesty of nature' that should be seen even in a typhoon. Much closer to haiku is the following from the 8th century *Seafarer:*

Storms there the stone-cliffs beat.
There them the starling answered, icy of wings,
Full oft the eagle screamed, dewy of wings.

Coming to the Middle English Period, the famous *Cuckoo Song* is almost pure haiku:

Sumer is icumen in,
Lhude sing cuccu!

'Sumer' here means rather spring. The important thing to notice is the imperative. Poetry is never merely indicative. The will of the poet is the will of nature, and every poetical sentence must have to some extent an imperative meaning. The word cuckoo itself is poetry, for the word is the thing. The cuckoo is its voice. When a cuckoo cuckoos we always have poetry. But how seldom does a human being human-be!

Chaucer sees nature only as a background for human life, and this goes for all the poets up to Sidney and beyond, but in the same century we have mystical writings that could have been the basis of haiku poetry, for example from *The Book of Privy Counselling,* apparently by the same author as *The Cloud of Unknowing:*

Let Him be only that He is as He is, and make Him no
otherwise. Seek no farther in Him by subtlety of wit.

This mystical attitude to God is the haiku poets' attitude to nature.

In the same 14th century again we find lines in *Winner and Waster* which may be paralleled in haiku:

> So sounded the rough streams,
> And reached so high,
> That it was nighing night
> Ere I nap might,
> For din of the deep waters
> And clamouring of birds.

A poet of the next century, who recently has become famous again, John Skelton, has many lines that are akin to haiku and senryu, for his verse, as he says himself, 'hath in it some pith'. Of his mistress's sparrow he writes like Issa:

> Sometimes he would gasp
> When he saw a wasp;
> A fly or gnat,
> He would fly at that;
> And prettily he would pant
> When he saw an ant;
> Lord, how he would pry
> After the butterfly!

A hundred years later Alexander Montgomery has a poem about the nightingale, which, when read with the Scots pronunciation, has the onomatopoeia which every good haiku should also have, especially with regard to (singing) birds:

> Thy chivring chirls whilk changingly thou chants,
> Makes all the rockes round thee ring.

Passing by Shakespeare and all the Elizabethan poets, we come to two Englishmen who if born in Japan would have been haiku poets, Herbert and Vaughan. In *Affliction,* Herbert writes:

> I read and sigh, and wish I were a tree
> For sure then I should grow
> To fruit or shade.

Again in *Employment:*

Oh that I were an orange-tree,
That busy plant!

Vaughan has the same feeling of the secondary importance of human beings
in his poem *Early Death*:

A *feather* or a *shell*,
A *stick*, or rod, which some chance brings,
The best of us excel.

Especially in *Eternim res creatae exerto capite observantes expectant
revelationem Filiorum Dei* (Romans VIII, 19) he not only repeats Herbert,

I would I were a stone, or tree,

but asserts that animals and plants and stones also have a sense of God, and
await the coming of Heaven on earth.

Cowper, in the 18th century, realised how poetic the trivia of life may be;
he has a great deal of what is called in haiku *jinji*, human affairs. Some of
Cowper's lines are haiku because of the pure sensation conveyed:

The poplars are fell'd; farewell to the shade
And the whispering sound of the cool colonnade.

Here sound and coolness and light and straightness are expressed concretely,
in two lines. However, Cowper's most charming lines, for instance

The squirrel, flippant, pert, and full of play,

and so on, are not haiku because they are, for all their aptness and humour,
mere pictures, like those of Milton with his larger brush.

It is with Thomson's *Seasons* (*Winter* was first, in 1726) that spring,
summer, autumn, winter really enter English poetry as subjects. Thomson
is too general for haiku, though we have such lines as:

And from the bladed field the fearful hare
Limps awkward.

We should not forget that Pope also, in spite of his poetic diction and dislike
of wild nature, taught his countrymen some things they needed to know, for
example:

Is it for thee, the lark ascends and sings?
Joy tunes his voice, joy elevates his wings!

And Gilbert White, the naturalist, writes of the swallows:

> I could not help being touched with a secret delight...to observe with
> how much ardour and punctuality those poor birds obeyed the strong
> impulse towards hiding.

Burns says, in one of his letters:

> I never hear the loud solitary whistle of the curlew in a summer noon,
> or the mild cadence of a troop of grey plovers in an autumn morning,
> without feeling an elevation of soul like the enthusiasm of devotion
> or poetry.

He states, without knowing he does so, that **the love of nature is religion,
and that religion is poetry; these three things are one thing.This is the
unspoken creed of the haiku poets.** However, when it becomes explicit, as
in Blake and the later Wordsworth, and often in Shelley, like every creed and
every dogma it has a stultifying, fossilising effect. In fact, one may say that
the better the belief the more harmful, since it is the more difficult to
disprove, and reprove.

Crabbe is the first English nature poet to realise that Nature is not, or
should not be, pretty, that the positive ugliness of a hippopotamus is far more
meaningful, that is, poetical, than the negative beauty of a butterfly. One
more example to add to those given before; Peter Grimes' haunt:

> Where the small eels that left the deeper way
> For the warm shore, within the shallows play;
> Where gaping mussels, left upon the mud,
> Slope their slow passage to the fallen flood.

Haiku poetesses are only fifth class, but Dorothy Wordsworth is superior
to her brother in some ways, in modesty, minuteness, and warmth. From the
Journal, May 6th 1802:

> The birch tree is all over green in *small* leaf, more light and elegant
> than when it is full out. It bent to the breezes, as if for the love of its
> own delightful motions.

Of Wordsworth it is not really necessary to say anything. *To the Cuckoo,
The Glow-worm, The Green Linnet, A Poet's Epitaph, To My Sister,* and a
dozen others are full of the spirit of haiku and nothing else. Even to the loose

pebble along the highway he 'gave a moral life', but he does not usually fall into moralising about nature. In the poetry of Wordsworth and that of haiku there is this seemingly unimportant but deeply significant common element: that the most ordinary people, those to whom Buddha preached and for whom Christ died, are able, if they will, to understand it.

Shelley's poetry has in it, in spite of his philosophising, an aspect of the Zen that is at the bottom of all haiku. Shelley's Zen and his point of contact with oriental ways of thinking come out clearly when we compare a phrase of Palgrave's, 'Shelley's wayward intensity', with the 'direction' of Chinese expression which Spengler says we see 'in free hither and thither wandering that nevertheless goes to the goal'. But the best and the last of the English nature poets is John Clare. The following, the final verse of [one of several of his poems entitled] *Autumn*, is three haiku:

> The feather from the raven's breast
> Falls on the stubble lea;
> The acorns near the old crow's nest
> Fall pattering down the tree;
> The grunting pigs, that wait for all,
> Scramble and hurry where they fall.

It would be wrong not to mention Thoreau here. His poetry is wooden, but *Walden* and *A Week on the Concord* are haibun if not haiku, in many places. He has always and everywhere, in every sentence, something that is essential to haiku, that is, humour. For example, from Sunday, in the *Week*:

> The meadows were a-drinking at their leisure; the frogs sat meditating, all Sabbath thoughts, summing up their week, with one eye out on the golden sun, and one toe upon a reed, eyeing the wondrous universe in which they act their part; the fishes swam more staid and soberly, as maidens go to church.

There were elements in the character of Keats which prevented him from writing much haiku poetry. For him, the object of life was a combination of love, fame, and poetry, though sometimes

> on the shore
> Of the wide world I stand alone, and think
> Till love and fame to nothingness do sink.

Even poetry, if pursued too vehemently, will shrivel, or worse still, putrify, for this 'poetry' is too much a matter of words, of trying to find the best word, instead of being satisfied with the right one. This we always feel, even in lines that are haiku-like:

                        a weeping cloud,
        That fosters the droop-headed flowers all
        And hides the green hill in an April shroud.

Clouds do not 'weep'. 'Fosters' does not harmonise with 'droop', and the word 'shroud', with its most unsuitable associations of death, is used for the rhyme. In the Buddhist *Ode to Melancholy* we have the transitoriness of life ('Beauty that must die') and the identity of opposites ('in the very temple of Delight, Veil'd Melancholy has her sovran shrine'), but it is in *Meg Merrilies,* his least typical poem, that we see the spirit of haiku, above all the spirit of Bashô:

        Her Brothers were the craggy hills,
        Her Sisters larchen trees—
        Alone with her great family
        She liv'd as she did please.

        No breakfast had she many a morn,
        No dinner many a noon,
        And, 'stead of supper she would stare
        Full hard against the Moon.

Where are love, fame, and poetry? In an unambitious sonnet, *On the Grasshopper and the Cricket,* we are reminded of the many good haiku on this subject in several lines:

                He has never done
        With his delights; or when tired out with fun,
        He rests at ease beneath some pleasant weed.

The last three lines of the *Ode to Autumn* are perhaps the best, the purest of all:
                and now with treble soft
        The red-breast whistles from a garden-croft;
        And gathering swallows twitter in the skies.

[   ] In the last hundred years, the nearest to haiku are Hardy and D. H. Lawrence. Hardy's novels contain passages of haibun, objective and lovingly exact, but without meaningless minutiae. They have humour, homeliness, warmth, and precision:

        The little birds in the hedges were rustling their feathers and tucking themselves in comfortably for the night, retaining their places if Oak kept moving, but flying away if he stopped to look at them.

Lawrence is too subjective for haiku; he hates so much in nature and will not resign himself to it, but the depth and intensity of his seeing into the life of things makes us wish to claim him as at least a heretic in the faith.

Through the open door, stealthily, came the scent of madonna lilies, almost as if it were prowling abroad. The moon was melting down upon the crest of the hill. It was gone; all was dark. The corncrake called still.

Just for good measure here are a few more examples of haiku in English literature put into the three-line form:

Hills of sheep,
And homes
Of the silent vanished races.

O lovely lily clean,
O lily springing green,
O lily bursting white!

Where the quick sandpipers flit
In and out the marl and grit,
That seems to breed them, brown as they.

Heavily hangs
The holly-hock,
Heavily hangs the tiger-lily. [   ]

While in a quiet mood
Hedge-sparrows try
An inward stir of shadowed melody.

The fair breeze blew,
The white foam flew,
The furrow followed free.

Enough examples have been given to show that even where English haiku lack a season word, when they are too long, or have too many adjectives, or tend to morality or emotionality, or philosophy, they have something in common with Japanese haiku. This common element is sense in thought, thought in sense; the thought is not mere thought, but the thought subsumed in sensation; the sensation is not simply sensation, but the sensation involved in real thinking, that is, poetical thinking. When they are divided or divisible, when the word and the object, the man and the thing are in any way separated or separable, no poetry, and especially that of haiku in any language, is possible.

(Two small quotations from 'History of Haiku' may be added here, and one from 'Japanese Life and Character in Senryu'.

> *Harukaze ya tôshi o dakite oka ni tatsu*
> The spring wind!
> With a fighting spirit
> I stand on the hill.   *Kyoshi*

This is a very Japanese verse. What the Japanese have is a feeling of fighting together with nature, never against it. [1]

Nature without man is a body without a soul. But when a particular man's feelings are inserted into nature, it is spoiled. Nature must be faintly suffused with humanity to give us complete satisfaction. [2]

Connected with the fact that the Japanese do not feel themselves in opposition to nature, that they do not wish to dominate it, is their making no division between what is good and what is beautiful. Truth is not seen as an external objective existence. The goal of life is not its attainment by slow and painful study. The truth is something created by us out of nothing at each moment. [3]

[1] *Vol. 2, Meiji Poets - I*
[2] *Vol. 1, Buson - I*
[3] *p.3*

9

HAIKU'S PLACE IN WORLD LITERATURE AND ITS TYPICAL SUBJECT MATTER

(This, the Preface to 'Haiku', Vol. 4, is dated Tokyo, 3 December, 1951.)

Japanese Literature stands or falls by haiku, in my opinion, but its unique characteristic makes it a difficult matter to assess its position in world literature. It is not merely the brevity by which it isolates a particular group of phenomena from all the rest; nor its suggestiveness, through which it reveals a whole world of experience. It is not only in its remarkable use of the season word, by which it gives us a feeling of a quarter of the year; nor its faint all-pervading humour. Its peculiar quality is its self-effacing, self-annihilative nature, by which it enables us, more than any other form of literature, to grasp the thing-in-itself. Just as we are to be in state of *muga,* self-lessness, when we compose haiku, so the haiku is not a thing of beauty and a joy for ever, but a finger-post, a raft unwanted when the river is crossed. If, like waka, the haiku itself has literary charm and value, we are distracted from the real region of haiku, the experience, the mutual, reunited life of poet and things.

The position which haiku has or should have in world literature may be brought out by comparing and contrasting Bashô with Shakespeare, Homer, Dante, Goethe and Cervantes. If he can hold his own with these, the 17-syllabled haiku may well claim an equality with the world masterpieces of epic, drama, and lyric.

Bashô has not the grim strength of Dante, but he also sees how

> The little flowers, bent and shut by the chill of night,
> Soon as the sunlight whitens them,
> Erect themselves quite open on their stems.
> *(Inferno II, ll.127-129)*

He has not Shakespeare's power to create forms more real than living man, but has the universality of

> Truly, sir, I am a poor fellow that would live,

as applied to all the things in the world, animate and inanimate:

> *Yoku mireba nazuna hana saku kakine kana*
> Looking carefully,—

> There is a shepherd's-purse
> Blooming under the hedge.

He has not Homer's grasp of the primitive nobility of men and women, but he has his pleasure in the plain and elemental things of life:

> *Mi ni shimite daikon karashi aki no kaze*
> In the bitter radish
> That bites into me, I feel
> The autumn wind.

Goethe's understanding of science was to Bashô unknown, but he shares with him the knowledge that there is nothing behind phenomena; 'they are themselves the meaning'. On the other hand, Bashô is an idealist like Cervantes, but he does not tilt at windmills either real or symbolical; he does something just as destructive however, in taking away from things their (apparent) heavy, stupid meaninglessness, and shows us them as the world of grace and nature in one.

In what point is Bashô equal or superior to these great men? In his touching the very nerve of life, his unerring knowledge of those moments in time which, put together, make up our real, our eternal life. He is awake in the world that for almost all men exists as a world of dreams.

Bashô gives us the same feeling of depth as Bach, and by the same means, not by noise and emotion as in Beethoven and Wagner, but by a certain serenity and 'expressiveness' which never aims at beauty but often achieves it, as it were by accident. This comparison between Bashô and Bach may seem to be far-fetched. They have little in common except their profound understanding of vital inevitability, and the meaning of death. As Confucius implies, he who understands either life or death, understands both. The hymn says, in its rather sentimental way,

> Days and moments, quickly flying,
> Blend the living with the dead,

and Bach and Bashô felt this so deeply that the average mind finds the one too intellectual and difficult, the other too simple.

Many people must have had the experience of reading haiku which have not seemed very good or striking, and yet, for some strange and unknown reason, were unforgettable. To take some examples; the first by Bashô:

> *Rokugatsu ya mine ni kumo oku Arashiyama*
> In the Sixth Month
> Mount Arashi
> Lays clouds on its summit.

To explain the poetic point of this would be very difficult. It lies partly, no doubt, in the personifying of the mountain, or rather, in realizing the 'life' of it, but the simple sublimity of the verse is Homeric; it is that of the cloud-capped mountain.

> *Inazuma ya kinô wa higashi kyô wa nishi*
> Summer lightning!
> Yesterday in the East,
> Today in the West.

There could be nothing less 'poetical' than this bald statement of meteorological fact by Kikaku, and yet we feel the vastness of nature, together with the underlying willing acceptance of man. The same is true of the following, by Yayû:

> *Futatsu mitsu hoshi miidasu ya naku kawazu*
> A few stars
> Are now to be seen,—
> And frogs are croaking.

Two or three stars have come out, dusk falling; a few frogs are croaking. The unity of nature is seen without a word about it; without, indeed, a glance at it.

There is a short poem by Robert Frost, *The Pasture,* that expresses to me almost the whole meaning of human life,—and with it the nature of haiku:

> I'm going out to clean the pasture spring;
> I'll only stop to rake the leaves away
> (And wait to watch the water clear, I may):
> I shan't be gone long. —You come too.
>
> I'm going out to fetch the little calf
> That's standing by the mother. It's so young
> It totters when she licks it with her tongue.
> I shan't be gone long.—You come too.

We see these things, the pasture spring and the water clearing, the cow and her wabbly calf, and in them our life is fulfilled, —but not entirely; you, the other person, humanity, must come too; myself and Nature and man, the tender and strong relation between us.

There are two elements in this relation, a systole and a diastole. There is eternity and infinity, and there are the 'minute particulars'. In life and art it is as well perhaps to allow the eternity and infinity to be overheard, overseen. **Where haiku is unrivalled is in its power of expressing the whole world of inanimate, or animate, or human life, and at the same time entering into the minutest details of fact or feeling.** The following example, by Bonchô, of this delicacy applies to visual sensations:

> *Hai sutete shiraume urumu kakine kana*
> Throwing away the ashes,
> The [line of] white plum-blossoms
> Became cloudy.

This does not mean that the blossoms became dirtied by the grey ash, nor does it mean that they became more beautiful. It is something between the two, leaning towards the second, but more indefinite, more hesitating than it. Not so delicate and more a matter of sensation, but still revealing the whole through the parts, a verse by Sodô:

> *Haru mo haya yamabuki shiroku chisha nigashi*
> Spring soon to be over,
> The yellow rose whitening,
> Lettuce becoming bitter.

Another example of the delicacy of the haiku poet is the following verse by Buson, where the feeling is quite a nameless one, without words to express it in any language, yet expressed, faultlessly and unequivocally:

> *Ume ochikochi minami subeku kita subeku*
> Plum-blossoms here and there,
> It is good to go north,
> Good to go south.

There is here a feeling of the newness of spring, and yet of the luxury, the bounty, the universality of the season; in truth, anywhere will do in these days of renewed life and beauty. One more example, also by Buson, in which the delicacy is so great as to require the maximum of effort on the part of the reader:

> *Na-no-hana ya hoshi ga yado wa towade sugi*
> Rape-flowers;

Not visiting the priest,
But passing by.

Buson is walking along a road on both sides of which rape-flowers are blooming. For some reason or other he passes by the monk's house he intended visiting. To say that he chooses nature instead of religion, the rape-flowers rather than talking with the monk,—this is not only saying too much, it is destroying the very life of the poetry which is in a realm that transcends (while including) this 'Shall I, or shall I not?' of hesitation and dubiety. There is a similar verse by Taigi:

> *Azamuite yukinuke tera ya oborozuki*
> Pretending it is on purpose,
> And passing through a temple,—
> The hazy moon.

Going out for a walk in the evening, the poet mistook the way and found himself in such a place that, to avoid going round a long way, he had to go through the temple grounds, so going in the gate, and bowing to the main temple and to the Buddhas enshrined in other buildings, he went out of the back gate, feeling that his religious actions had been more than usually spiced with practical requirements and hypocritical observances. And the moon, quite properly, is hazy. The tenderness of mind which is the most prominent characteristic of the writer of haiku is distinctly (almost too distinctly) seen in the following verse by Shiki:

> *Nata agete kiran to sureba konome kana*
> Lifting up the hatchet
> To cut it down,—
> It was budding.

This has been compared to the verse by Meisetsu, composed thirteen years later:

> *Kama o togeba akaza kanashimu keshiki ari*
> Sharpening the sickle,
> The goose-foot [1]
> Looks as if grieving.

Though haiku are so restricted in their subject matter, we have no feeling of monotony as we read them. There are however five main types: verses that record sensations; pictures of life; self-portrayals; verses that express human warmth; and romantic verses.

[1] *Named from the shape of the leaves.*

1. Examples of sensation

> *Asasamu ya tabi no yado tatsu hito no koe*
> Morning cold;
> The voices of travellers
> Leaving the inn.

The voice of the men who are setting out early this autumn morning, and the coldness of the air, reinforce each other. The sound is clearer, chillier; the cold has a human meaning. There is another verse by the same author, Taigi, but the time is evening:

> *Tabibito ya yosamu toiau nebuta-goe*
> Travellers,
> Asking about the cold at night,
> In sleepy voices.

> *Musubu yori haya ha ni hibiku izumi kana*
> On the point of scooping up the water,
> I felt it in my teeth,—
> The water of the spring.

To Bashô, it was not merely the sight of the cold water but the action of putting the hands together to scoop it up that caused the strength of the sensation of chill in his teeth. The following is by Shikô:

> *Uma no mimi subomete samushi nashi no hana*
> The horse lays back his ears;
> Flowers of the pear-tree
> Are chill and cold.

The flowers of the pear, unlike those of the cherry and plum, have no brilliancy or gaiety, but rather some loneliness and melancholy. The horse on his way home this cold spring evening puts back his ears, and they are in momentary accord with the flowers.

> *Ume no hana akai wa akai wa akai wa na*
> These flowers of the plum,—
> How red, how red they are,
> How red, indeed!

Also by Izen, a contemporary of Bashô famous for his doctrine of spontaneity, the two following verses:

Isogiwa ni zaburi zaburi to nami uchite
Along the sea-shore
Fall the waves, fall and hiss,
Fall and hiss.

Sugi no ki ni sû sû kaze no fukiwatari
Through the cedars
Whew, whew, whew,
Whistles the breeze.

The next two are by Issa:

Futatsu naki kasa nusumareshi doyô kana
The hottest day of the year;
The only *kasa* I had,—
Stolen!   (*kasa* = hat)

We have here the inhumanity of man added to the inhumanity of nature. Issa
nearly always gives us this, and in the following also:

Atsuki yo no ni to ni no aida ni netarikeri
A hot night;
Sleeping in between
The bags and baggages.

2. Pictures of life

Meigetsu ya funamushi hashiru ishi no ue
The bright autumn moon:
Sea-lice running
Over the stones.

This verse, by Tôrin, is peculiarly vivid and mobile. The moonlight is so
bright that we can see even the sea-lice running about on their business over
the stones left dry by the falling tide. But in some way or other we feel that
the moonlight has itself come alive in the silvery creatures that move so
smoothly here and there. The stones too share in this light-life. The first of
the two following verses is by Raizan, the second by Bashô:

Harukaze ya shirasagi shiroshi matsu no naka
In the spring breeze
The snowy heron flies white
Among the pine-trees.

Suzume to koe nakikawasu nezumi no su
Baby mice in their nest
Squeak in response
To the young sparrows.

The young mice in the ceiling and the young sparrows under the eaves are both chirping. These so different forms of life have the same pathos and faint humour of all incomplete things. Bashô, like Wordsworth, is saying,

I have heard the call
Ye to each other make.

The following verses, the first by Gojô, the second by Kozan, go beyond mere pictures; they have three or more dimensions.

Natsukusa ya yamadera michi no ishibotoke
Summer grasses;
Along the path to the mountain temple,
Stone images of Buddha.

Stone Buddhas line the path to the temple in the mountains, almost unseen until we turn a sharp corner, and one of the images gives us a profound impression of the divine in nature, part of it, and yet above and beyond it.

Hototogisu yoru wa ki o kiru oto mo nashi
A *hototogisu* sings
Among the evening shades;
No sound of the woodcutter.   (*hototogisu* = small cuckoo)

This absence of things never fails to deepen the meaning of those that remain. The verse actually says: 'No sound of wood-cutting'.

Aonori ya ishi no kubomi no wasure-jio
Green seaweed;
In the hollows of the rocks,
The forgotten tide.

This verse belongs to spring; the following, also by Kitô, to summer:

Yamadera ya en no shita naru koke shimizu
A mountain temple;
Clear water running under the verandah,
Moss at the sides.

For a poet, or a child, this is the ideal dwelling place. The following, by Seira, has the simplicity of W.H.Davies:

> *Tsuno agete ushi hito o miru   natsuno kana*
> Lifting up their horns,
> The cattle look at people
> On the summer moor.

The grass is rank, the day hot, the cattle moving slowly with their heads down. When someone approaches them they raise their heads, or rather, they raise their horns above the tall grasses, and we feel something menacing yet mild that tells of the wonder and power and danger of nature.

> *Tagayasu ya tori sae nakanu yamakage ni*
> Tilling the field,
> Not even a bird cries
> In the shadow of the hill.

In this verse, by Buson, we feel the season, the beginning of April, the lateness of the coming of warmth here under the hill-side, the young leaves unfolding, no breeze, complete silence,—and with all this, the softly-harsh sound of the hoe. The following verse, by Shirô, is at the opposite extreme:

> *Tôtô to taki no ochikomu shigeri kana*
> The waterfall
> Thunders down
> Into the rank leaves.

The tremendous rush of water and tumultuous sounds have their correspondence in the wildly growing plants and weeds and trees all around.

> *Chô no ha no ikutabi koyuru hei no yane*
> How many butterflies
> Winged their way across
> This roofed wall!

What struck Bashô was not merely the contrast between the wings of the lightly flying butterflies and the heavily tiled earthen wall, but the way in which they appear from the unknown, and disappear into it with that levity and aimless purposefulness that characterise them. The following, by Gyôdai, is a wonderful and powerful verse:

Akatsuki ya kujira no hoeru shimo no umi
In the dawn
Whales roaring;
A frosty sea.

The beginning of day, the spouting of the whales, the sea, the frost,—all these have something primitive and primaeval in them.

Sayo shigeru tonari no usu wa hikiyaminu
The people next door
Have stopped grinding the mortar:
Cold rain at night.

The connection between one thing and another is always incredibly strange, even when it is simple cause and effect. How much more so here, where the mere cessation of one sound causes Yaha now to understand the meaning of the rain that has been falling all the time. Compare the following by Bonchô:

Akuoke no shizuku yamikeri kirigirisu
The drip-drip
Of the lye-bucket ceases:
The voice of the cricket.

The following three verses, by Uryû, Gusai, and Kikaku, bring out well the vitality and variety of haiku:

Koi no oto mizu honoguraku ume shiroshi
The sound of the carp,
The water faintly dark,
The plum-blossoms white.

Ôdera no tobira aketaru haruhi kana
A spring day;
They open the folding-doors
Of the great temple.

Koko kashiko kawazu naku yo ya hoshi no kage
Here and there
Frogs croaking in the night,
Stars shining.

The following small picture of country life by Bashô is more of sound than of sight. The one after that, by Gyôdai, is larger:

Niwatori no koe ni shigururu ushiya kana
Winter rain falling
On the cow-shed;
The voice of the cock.

Hi kuretari Miidera kudaru haru no hito
The day darkening,
They come down from Mii Temple,
People of the spring.

We see here the shades of evening falling over a wide scene, Lake Biwa in the distance, the Temple above, the long flight of stone steps, and in ones and twos, people who are reluctantly leaving the cherry-blossoms behind, so aptly termed 'people of the spring'.

Hito mo minu haru ya kagami no ura no ume
A spring unseen of men,—
On the back of the mirror
A flowering plum-tree.

This verse by Bashô is one that Keats would have appreciated. There is a world of art which hardly belongs to this world except as a kind of perversion of it, a sort of back-of-the-mirror which our mind holds up to nature. This is the world that Bashô was also drawn to, but like Wordsworth, the real world was the one he earnestly desired to live in.

Uguisu ya geta no ha ni tsuku oda no tsuchi
The *uguisu*!
Earth of the rice-fields sticks
On the supports of the clogs.   (*uguisu* = bush warbler)

Two extremes of the whole of spring are given here by Bonchô, the heavenly voice of the *uguisu*, and the mud on the two 'teeth' of the *geta*, or wooden clogs.

Hototogisu naku ya ko-no-ma no sumi-yagura
A *hototogisu* cries;
Between the trees
A corner turret.

The bird suddenly cried, and looking round, Shihô saw through a gap in the trees, the white corner of the donjon silhouetted against the blue sky of summer.

100

Mame ueru hata mo kibeya mo meisho kana
Fields for sowing beans,
Firewood sheds,—
All famous places.

This was written by Bonchô at Rakushisha, in Saga, Kyorai's villa, where Kobori Enshû, a great landscape gardener, had his tea-ceremony house. These fields sown with beans, sheds for firewood, were once scenes of splendour and of the cultural life of the community. Both the glory and the misery of human existence are powerfully contrasted.

Kogarashi ya mabataki shigeki neko no tsura
In the winter storm
The cat keeps on
Blinking its eyes.

This by Yasô is on the one hand a vivid picture of the cat, its hatred of wind and confusion, the ears back, head down, blinking its half-shut eyes. On the other hand it is a description of one aspect of the essential nature of the winter wind,— its make-cats-blink-ness.

Waka-ayu ya tani no kozasa mo hitoha yuku
With the young trout in the valley
A leaf of the dwarf bamboo
Floats away.

If we take this as a real experience of Buson, we cannot help admiring the presence of mind (of Mind) that could seize such a moment, such a world of meaning in miniature. If we take it, as some do, as pure imagination, we shall be even more struck by Buson's power of pictorial creation.

Shizukasa ya kosui no soko no kumo no mine
The stillness;
Peaks of cloud
In the bosom of the lake.

We are reminded of Wordsworth's lines:

that uncertain heaven received
Into the bosom of the steady lake.

In Issa's verse we have rest only; in Wordsworth there is both motion and rest.

The next is by the same author.

> *Nadeshiko ya Jizô Bosatsu no atosaki ni*
> Before and behind
> Jizô Bosatsu,
> Pinks are blooming.

Jizô is the patron of travellers and children, and his statue is often found at cross-roads and other lonely places. His relation to the pinks may be taken in either of two ways: the sweetness of Jizô and the pinks; and the contrast between his calm indifference and their eager little faces.

> *Shiratsuyu ya imo no hatake no amanogawa*
> White dew;
> Over the potato field
> The Milky Way.

The Milky Way is the dew of heaven; the dew on the potato leaves is the stars of this earth. But as so often, there is something a little dead about Shiki's still-lifes. The next is better.

> *Yûdachi ya suna ni tsukitatsu aomatsuba*
> A summer shower;
> Green pine-needles
> Stick in the sand.

We feel here the force of the shower, that breaks off the pine-needles and thrusts them into the sand, so that they stand up in it.

> *Kiri no ha wa ochitsukusu naru o mokufuyô*
> The leaves of the paulownia
> Having all fallen,—
> The tree-lotus in bloom.

When the great leaves of the paulownia have all fallen, it is late autumn, but just at this time the flowers of the tree-lotus bloom. There is sometimes an unnaturalness about nature which makes her akin to us.

The above and all the remaining verses of this second section are by Buson.

> *Ike to kawa hitotsu ni narinu haru no ame*
> In the spring rain,
> The pond and the river
> Have become one.

102

We have here the omnipresence and omnipotence of water; and realize that what seemed three different things, lake, stream, and rain, are intrinsically one.

> *Nowaki yande nezumi no wataru nagare kana*
> The autumn storm
> Stopped blowing;
> A rat swam over the stream.

Though he has not Bashô's mysticism or Issa's humanity, Buson is not shallow, however. It is Nature without God or man, but not that of science. As so often in Thoreau, Nature speaks for herself.

> *Furuido no kuraki ni otsuru tsubaki kana*
> A camellia;
> It fell into the darkness
> Of an old well.

This has something deeply symbolical in it,—but we are not to think of what, just to feel it so, and stop there.

> *Kishine yuku ho wa osoroshiki wakaba kana*
> Passing the bank,
> [Fearful for the sail:]
> The young leaves!

This literal translation of the original shows the way in which the speed of the boat and the luxuriance of the young leaves are seen as aspects of one awful energy of nature.

> *Ugoku ha mo nakute osoroshi natsu kodachi*
> How awesome!
> Not a leaf stirs
> In the summer grove!

The feeling seems to belong rather to tropical forests; it reminds one of W. H. Hudson's stories of South America.

> *Mijikayo no yo no ma ni sakeru botan kana*
> The short night;
> The peony opened
> During that time.

In this verse Buson has expressed the power of nature that can make the great flower bloom in such a short time as the summer night.

> *Aoume o   uteba katsu chiru aoba kana*
> Beating down the green plums,
> As, at the same time,
> Green leaves fall.

This is a good example of how nothing escapes the eye of the haiku poet, and how this slight accompanying fact of some leaves being knocked down too is perceived as deeply significant of the way in which purpose and accident are mingled in our world.

> *Soko miete uo miete aki no mizu fukashi*
> The bottom seen clearly,
> The fish seen clearly,—
> Deep is the water of autumn.

Not only is the sky of autumn high, the water is deep. There seems to be a double infinity in this season, one above us, one below. Compare the following; the season is summer:

> *Hitokuchi ni   taranu shimizu no   tôtosa yo*
> The clear water,
> Not enough for a mouthful,—
> But how wonderful!

Thoreau says: 'The shallowest still water is unfathomable'.

> *Shizuka naru kaki-no-ki-hara ya   fuyu no tsuki*
> How calm
> The persimmon orchard
> Under the wintry moon!

Dorothy Wordsworth notes in her *Journal*, 24th March, 1798:

> The crooked arm of the old oak-tree points upwards to the moon.

Tachigare no ki ni semi nakite kumo no mine
A tree stands withered,
And on it a cicada crying;
Billowing clouds.

This verse seems to be one of contrast; contrast between the bare, wintry angularity of the tree with the shrill-crying insect, and the softly-swelling clouds that rise up in the summer sky; or perhaps the cicada unites with its hard warmth the tree and the clouds.

U-no-hana no koboruru fuki no hiroha kana
The flowers of the *u*
Spill on the broad leaves
Of the bog-rhubarb.

The small white, snow-like flowers of the *u* fall on the round, dark leaves of the bog-rhubarb.

Oshidori ya itachi no nozoku ike furushi
Mandarin ducks;
A weasel is peeping
At the old pond.

Compare Shiki's verse, which seems a more homely version:

Kiku arete niwatori nerau itachi kana
The chrysanthemums withering,
A weasel is watching
The hens.

There are two more verses by Buson that we may give here; the first belongs to summer, the second to spring:

Meshi nusumu kitsune oiutsu mugi no aki
Driving away with blows
A fox stealing the rice;
The autumn of barley.

Everyone is out in the summer fields, and the fox comes to the kitchen. In the following there is a contrast between the fine threads of rain and the broad expanse of water, and a harmony in their mild vagueness:

Harusame no naka o nagaruru taiga kana
Flowing through the midst
Of the spring rain,
A great river.

3. Self-portrayals In the following verses the poets are speaking to some
extent of themselves; Onitsura's haiku is well-known:

Gyôzui no sutedokoro nashi mushi no koe
The bath water,—
Where can I throw it away?
The voices of insects.

The hesitation and at-a-loss-ness of the poet is heightened by the fact that he
cannot see the insects, he can only hear their sweet voices trilling out from
every bush and plant. The immaterial conquers the material, men do not live
by bread alone. There is a waka [tanka] by Kageki, 1768 - 1843, very
similar in meaning, but more aristocratic in mind-colour:

Izuku yori koma uchi-iremu Sahogawa no
sazare ni utsuru shiragiku no hana
Whence shall I ride my horse
Into the River Saho?
White chrysanthemums
Are reflected
On the pebbles.

Yasezune no ke ni bifû ari koromogae
A breeze blowing
On the hairs on thin shanks:
The change of clothes.

This, by Buson, is one of those verses which make us wonder at the
delicacy of the poetical mind of the Japanese, and their faith in what is small
and insignificant. In *Moby Dick,* Melville says:

We expand to bulk. To produce a mighty volume you must have a
mighty theme. No great and enduring volume can be written on the
flea, though many there be who have tried it.

This is true, but it is not the only truth. The hairs on the legs of the man who
has put on his new spring clothes has a meaning, a slender rapier-like
meaning that is 'not as big as a barn door,—but 'twill suffice'. Tu Fu says:

When one petal flies away, spring is over.

Tori morotomo no ni deshi ware mo kasumuran
Out in the fields
Together with the birds,
I will be surrounded with mist.

Chora walks the fields. He also could say, no doubt,[with Marvell]

Casting the body's vest aside,
My soul into the boughs does glide;
There like a bird it sits, and sings,
Then whets, and combs its silver wings,

but to say so seems somehow to spoil it. Together with the birds he will be surrounded by the morning mist. That is enough.

Dai no ji ni nete suzushisa yo sabishisa yo
Lying with arms and legs outstretched,
How cool,—
How lonely!

When we are alone, we can do as we like, lie as we please; but this is, as Issa says, because we are alone.

Yo no natsu ya kosui ni ukabu nami no ue
Summer in the world;
Floating on the waves
Of the lake.

This verse by Bashô reminds us of Thoreau, with his power of feeling and portraying the present and the past, the near and the far, in one place, at one moment.

Ware shinaba hakamori to nare kirigirisu
Grasshopper!
Be the keeper of the grave-yard,
When I die.

This verse contains everything of Issa, his feeling of impermanence, of kinship with other creatures, and the all-pervading humour. The same may be said of the following, but the humour is fainter:

Ikite iru bakari zo ware to keshi no hana
Just simply alive,
Both of us, I
And the poppy.

Issa was the most democratic man (or should one say 'biocratic'?) who ever lived. More implicit still is the next verse:

Chô ga kite tsurete yuki keri niwa no chô
A butterfly came
And flew off
With a butterfly in the garden.

Takegari ya tô o agureba mine no tsuki
Mushroom-hunting;
Raising my head,—
The moon over the peak.

This verse of Buson, which shows that dusk has fallen unawares, is quite different from Li Po's:

I raise my head, and gaze at the moon over the mountains;
I lower my head, and think of my native place.

Buson's verse simply describes the two worlds, that of minute particulars near the eye, and that of the vast and distant.

Kochira muke ware mo sabishiki aki no kure
Turn this way;
I also am lonely,
This evening of autumn.

Unchiku, a monk of Kyoto, seems to have painted a picture of himself with his face turned away, and asked Bashô to write a verse on it. Bashô said, 'You are sixty and I nearly fifty already. Both of us, in a dream-world, are portraying a dream. To this (picture of a dream) I add this somniloquy.' In this verse we see more strongly than in perhaps any other verse the intense subjectivity of Bashô's mind. Even a few smears of ink on a piece of paper, and he feels our loneliness, our isolation in the sea of life,

The unplumb'd, salt, estranging sea.

So he begs the monk in the picture not to turn his face from him in the evening twilight.

4. Verses that express human warmth. Bashô and Issa are the poets of humanity. The following is by the former:

> *Tsukishiro ya hiza ni te o oku yoi no uchi*
> The moon about to appear,
> All present tonight
> With their hands on their knees.

This is a verse praising the moon through a picture of the poets and moon-lovers who are gathered to gaze at it. The moon has not yet risen, but all are sitting waiting. Bashô glances mildly round, and notices that each man has his hands on his knees, a form of polite deportment. In the hands is seen the minds of those present; in the hands the moon too is seen, the yet invisible moon that whitens the horizon above the dark mountains in the distance. Hardy's *The Oxen* strongly reminds us of Bashô's haiku.

> Christmas Eve, and twelve of the clock.
> 'Now they are all on their knees',
> An elder said as we sat in a flock
> By the embers in hearthside ease.

> We pictured the meek mild creatures where
> They dwelt in their strawy pen,
> Nor did it occur to one of us there
> To doubt they were kneeling then.

> *Tama-arare yotaka wa tsuki ni kaerumeri*
> Hail-stones on the ground;
> The 'night hawks' come back home
> In the moonbeams.

'Night-hawks' were the lowest kind of prostitute in Edo. They appeared after dark, carrying straw mats. Issa is sleeping alone in the cold, and hears them walking by or talking. He also knows what cold and hunger and suffering mean, and the softness of the language he uses, *kaerumeri,* shows his compassionate feeling.

> *Ko ga kurete chatsumi mo kiku ya hototogisu*
> Do the tea-pickers also,
> Hidden in the bushes,
> Hear the *hototogisu*?

The tea-trees are quite high, and women picking the tea-leaves can hardly be seen, only the towels on their heads, or their faces and hands occasionally visible. The *hototogisu* is singing, and Bashô is thinking, not of himself, but of humanity, of those hardly-to-be-seen workers in the bushes,—are they too entering into their heritage of poetic life as the notes of the *hototogisu* ripple over the field?

> *Keisei no hata mitagaruru sumire kana*
> These violets!
> How the courtesans must want
> To see the spring fields!

The courtesans of Edo were never allowed out of the enclosure. Ryôto sees a distant connection of grace between the violets and the women.

> *Samidare ya shikishi hegitaru kabe no ato*
> Falling summer rain;
> Walls with their remaining
> Pictures peeling.

This verse comes in the *Saga Diary*, 1691, being written after Bashô had looked through each room of a small house for the Tea Ceremony, Rakushisha, 'falling persimmon hut', [ ] a temporary residence of Bashô's pupil Kyorai. On the walls of these rooms were once put paintings and sketches. Now faded and stained, they are seen in the half-darkness of the summer rains. Bashô and the rain and the dark, damp rooms with their discoloured walls are indeed in harmony. The following five verses are by Buson, showing the humanity of the artist-poet, much greater than usually supposed:

> *Yuku ware ni todomaru nare ni aki futatsu*
> I go;
> Thou stayest:
> Two autumns.

The Japanese has seventeen syllables, the English only eight, but the whole of life is given here, our meetings, our partings, the world of nature we each live in, different yet the same.

> *Akindo ni yukichigôtaru natsuno kana*
> The travelling pedlar;
> Passing each other
> On the summer moor.

Buson here expresses (by not expressing) that faint feeling of sympathy and respect we have for man in his struggle with heat and weight and loneliness and poverty.

Meigetsu ya aruji o toeba imohori ni
The harvest moon;
Calling on the master of the house,
He was digging potatoes.

The bright moon, the dark earth, the dully gleaming potatoes, and his friend who is enjoying the moon in the English way, digging the field in the moonlight. A stage lower:

Gôriki wa tada ni misuginu yamazakura
The mountain guide
Simply takes no notice
Of the cherry-blossoms.

There is something good in this too, the animal indifference that takes beauty for granted.

Byônin no kago mo sugikeru mugi no aki
A palanquin passes,
With a sick man in it:
The autumn of barley.

'Barley's autumn' is summer. The farmers are cutting and threshing and stacking the barley; all is bustle and energy and healthy activity in the sunshine. But as the pale, sick man is slowly carried through their midst, they realise that the world is larger and darker than they thought.

Suzukaze ya chikara ippai kirigirisu
A cool breeze,
The grasshopper singing
With all his might.

What is interesting here is Issa's conscious subjectivity. He attributes his own feeling of coolness to the grasshopper, who sings so joyfully 'under some pleasant weed'.

5. Examples of romantic verses. The following is by Bashô, whose verses are more various than usually thought:

Chô tori no shiranu hana ari aki no sora
A flower unknown
To bird and butterfly,—
The sky of autumn.

In *The Story of My Heart,* Richard Jefferies writes:

> The rich blue of the unattainable flower of the sky drew my soul
> towards it, and there it rested, for pure colour is rest of heart.

> *Kagiri aru inochi no hima ya aki no kure .*
> Autumn evening:
> Life has its limits,
> But its moments too of leisure.

We live in time, but also in eternity. This short autumn evening is for Buson
one of these moments, moments of vision, 'spots of time' Wordsworth calls
them. Or Thoreau:

> Now chiefly is my natal hour,
> And only now my prime of life.
> I will not doubt the love untold,
> Which not my worth nor want has bought,
> Which wooed me young and woos me old,
> And to this evening hath me brought.

> *Ran no ka ya chô no tsubasa ni takimono su*
> The butterfly is perfuming
> Its wings, in the scent
> Of the orchid.

This verse was composed by Bashô in response to a request by a Miss
Butterfly of a tea-house he stopped at on the way back from visiting Ise
Shrine. It was once the custom of ladies of high rank to perfume their clothes
in the smoke of certain scented trees such as sandal-wood.

> *Koe karete saru no ha shiroshi mine no tsuki*
> Its voice hoarsening,
> The white teeth of the monkey
> In the moon over the peak.

This was written by Kikaku about a place in China, Bachiang, famous for its
screaming monkeys. Its romantic, 'poetical' flavour may be contrasted with
Bashô's homely, everyday verse:

> *Shiodai no haguki mo samushi uo no tana*
> In the fish-shop
> The gums of the salt bream
> Look cold.

In the next example, however, Bashô is once more romantic:

> *Tsuki izuko kane wa shizumite umi no soko*
> Where is the moon?
> The bell is sunk
> At the bottom of the sea.

This was written on the fifteenth of the month, at the time of the full moon, when it was obscured by rain, at Tsuruga. The host told them that there was a story that in the sea a temple bell had sunk and that it could not be raised because it had sunk upside down. Bashô uses this legend, found in various parts of the world, to bring out the unseen beauty and mystery of the moon in the poetical mind.

> *Koishinaba waga tsuka de nake hototogisu*
> Should I die of love,
> O *hototogisu,*
> Cry at my tomb!

This verse is well-known from its being written by a woman, Ôshu, said to have been a courtesan of the Yoshiwara in Edo. There is something Elizabethan about it, reminding one of

> Come away, come away, death,

and other lyrics. This haiku belongs to the world of the mind rather than that of the body, and is about to bid adieu to the real, the poetical world, but with such a pang as moves us in spite of ourselves.

Enough examples have been given perhaps to show that haiku are infinitely varied within their very limited scope. Somehow or other, when we read them, all the important things they omit, sex, war, and the struggle for existence generally, do not seem to matter quite so much after all. There is a repose, a serenity about them which makes the tragedies of life and art seem somewhat hysterical, somewhat vulgar.

To conclude this over-long preface, I would like to say something about the translation of haiku into English, taking as an example the most famous of all, Bashô's *Furu-ike ya kawazu tobikomu mizu no oto.* This I translated [elsewhere] as follows:

113

The old pond;
A frog jumps in,—
The sound of the water.

The three-line translation used in these volumes obscures something fundamental in the originals, something that belongs to the Japanese mind, the Japanese language and the literature it produced and which produced it. We see it in linked poems, in the puns of the language of Nô, in the empty spaces of pictures, the absence of things in rooms, the silences of conversation. This 'something' is a certain continuity, a lack of division, a feeling of the whole when dealing with the parts.

In the present haiku, the first line, that is, the first five syllables, are 'end-stopped' by the particle *ya*, which we can represent only by a semicolon, since 'ah' is sentimental, 'yes' too much like smacking the lips, and an exclamation mark just ridiculous. But the second and third lines, that is, the middle seven and final five syllables, may either be divided, as in the above translation, or taken continuously. The verb *tobikomu,* 'jumps in', has also an adjectival function, qualifying *oto,* 'sound', thus meaning, 'the water jumped into by a frog'. We may therefore translate the verse as follows:

The old pond;
The sound
Of a frog jumping into the water.

But besides looking a bit odd, this translation, though undoubtedly nearer to the original than the former one, isolates the sound from the rest of the elements of the experience and makes it subsidiary to them. A point of interest and importance is whether the verse is one of sound only, or of sight and sound. Did Bashô see the frog jump in, and hear the sound of the water? This seems rather matter-of-fact. Did he hear the sound, and deduce the frog from past experience, or a balance of probabilities? This is too rational and logical. Bashô's real, that is, ideal experience must have been that represented by the following:

The old pond;
The-sound-of-a-frog-jumping-into-the-water.

But even this is too exact, too definite, too much of a complete and grammatical whole. The original haiku is more fragmentary; it is indeed just a link or two of what Pater calls 'the great chain wherewith we are bound'.
[   ]

*(More on **Furu-ike ya**, from 'Zen in English Literature and Oriental Classics', Chapter 15.)*

The most famous of all haiku, of which I give an unconventional translation, has this same quality, that is, of expressing an unsymbolical, unallegorical fact, which is nevertheless a Fact, and The Fact.

> The old pond.
> A frog jumps in—
> Plop!

Against this translation it may be urged that 'plop' is an un-poetical, rather humorous word. To this I would answer, 'Read it over slowly, about a dozen times, and this association will disappear largely'. Further, it may be said, the expression 'plop' is utterly different in sound from *'mizu no oto'*. This is not quite correct. The English 'sound of the water' is too gentle, suggesting a running stream or brook. The Japanese word *'oto'* has an onomatopoeic value much nearer to 'plop'. Other translations are wide of the mark. 'Splash' sounds as if Bashô himself had fallen in. Yone Noguchi's 'List, the water sound', shows Bashô in a graceful pose with finger in air. 'Plash', by Henderson, is also a misuse of words. Anyway, it is lucky for Bashô that he was born a Japanese, because probably not even he could have said it in English. Now we come to the meaning. An English author writes as follows:

> Some scholars maintain that this haiku about the frog is a perfect philosophical comment on the littleness of human life in comparison with the infinite. Such poems are hints, suggestions, rather than full expressions of an idea.

No haiku is a philosophical comment. Human life is not little: it is not to be compared with the infinite, whatever that is. Haiku are not hints; they suggest nothing whatever.

One of the great merits of this poem is that it lends itself to almost any interpretation that may be put upon it. But in general these may be reduced to four:

1. It is an ordinary poem of no special merit. This modern view allows it historic importance, and marks for its objectivity.

2. It is an expression of silence and serenity, accentuated in prospect and retrospect by the sound of the water made by the frog. This, I think we may say, is the impression made on the average reader who has some appreciation of Bashô's way of life.

3. It is a symbolic and mystical poem. The sound of the water is the Voice of God, 'old' means timeless, the pond is infinity, the plunging of the frog into the water is the baptism of the soul in death, the death of the self. (To be quite honest, I must say that I have just invented this interpretation myself.) Almost all Japanese would recoil from this instinctively. When I translated what I have just written, to my wife, she said, 'It reminds me somehow of the Olympic Games', and this is the reaction of a healthy, lively mind to such a false and forced explanation. God, eternity, infinity, death, the soul,—such conceptions are possible though hardly attractive subjects for haiku, but as stated above, haiku are not hints, they do not suggest such notions to us.

4. D.T. Suzuki relates the story of this haiku being an answer to the question 'What is reality?', but this seems as apocryphal as that of Kikaku's suggesting *The yellow rose* as the first part of the poem and Bashô's rejection of it. Suzuki further says, 'The source of life has been grasped', and this is no doubt true, and it is equally true of all poetry, all art, all music, though the grasping has different degrees of strength and persistence. The danger of this view is that it makes this poem stink of Zen.

10

MORE ABOUT 'FOUND HAIKU' IN ENGLISH POETRY

(Blyth illustrates this chapter, from 'Haiku', Vol 1, with examples under a variety of headings : Spring, The Lark, The Cock, Summer, Autumn, The Waterfowl, Winter. Under Autumn alone, poets he instances include Mary Robinson, Masefield, Coleridge, Francis Thompson, Whitman, Lowell, Arnold, Tennyson, Sidney, Susan Gaspell, Thoreau, de la Mare, Langston Hughes, Landor, Sassoon, William Morris, and of course Wordsworth. Regrettably, there is not space for examples here, and we hope that those in Section 8.5 may suffice.)

In *Zen in English Literature* examples were given from the whole range of English literature of the spirit of Zen which infuses it. Wherever there is the spirit of haiku, there is Zen, but the reverse is not true, for Zen may be diffused throughout long passages, or, on the other hand, be contained in a single word or phrase that in its brevity of utterance and length of context transcends the power of the seventeen syllables of haiku.

Proverbs, in poetry certain phrases, in prose a stray sentence here and there,—these correspond to haiku in the sense of being the peaks of poetic feeling and insight. Coleridge says, in *Biographia Litteraria,*

A poem of any length neither can be, nor ought to be, all poetry.

Pater, in his essay on *Wordsworth,* after pointing out the necessity of a selection of the poems of Wordsworth, speaks of his many prosaic poems, which yet contain

the few perfect lines, the phrase, the single word, perhaps,

which represents the moment of enthusiasm, of divine possession. Besides the question of length, there is that of aim, and we find something about a great deal of English poetry that is faintly repulsive to a delicate feeling. Especially where there is a striving after effect, the exquisite epithet, the bowel-stirring last line, we feel a desire to give up all literature and return to things themselves, things which never say more than they are, which are never understatements with an ulterior motive.

Only we'll sit upon the daisied grass,
And hear the larks and see the swallows pass;

Only we'll live awhile, as children play,
Without tomorrow, without yesterday.[1]

     Haiku are not these peaks of strenuous poetic effort; they are not the cream of a Western verse. There is something spontaneous, effortless, something even flat about them; but this flatness also comes unsought for. It is emotion recollected in moments of *tranquillity*—this is what is overlooked by so many poets. This tranquillity of the poet is an essential element, for it corresponds to the tranquillity, the point of rest, of all living things. The haiku poet also

remembers
The beauty of fire from the beauty of embers. [2]

[ ] Haiku or something like them, may be found scattered throughout English prose, perhaps more frequently than in poetry, where the tension and intention are so much greater. [ ]

[1] *Mary P. Robinson, Let us Forget.*   [2] *Masefield, On Growing Old.*

THE STATE OF MIND FOR HAIKU

(In 'Haiku', Vol. 1., Section 2, Blyth names thirteen 'characteristics of the state of mind which the creation and appreciation of haiku demand'. They are given below.)

1. Selflessness.
2. Loneliness.
3. Grateful acceptance.
4. Wordlessness.
5. Non-intellectuality.
6. Contradictoriness.
7. Humour.
8. Freedom.
9. Non-morality.
10. Simplicity.
11. Materiality.
12. Love.
13. Courage.

ON HAIGA

(Haiga are compositions in which poetry, calligraphy, and painting, or drawing, complement each other, blending together in the spontaneousness of their execution and the compression of their style. Haiga had an enormous appeal for Blyth. Sadly, the exigencies of this publication have forced us to exclude reproductions of haiga [1] *but we hope this paragraph, from 'History of Haiku', Vol. 2, will lead the reader on a self-managed quest to find out more about them.)*

[Like] haiku and the art of Tea, and Flower-arrangement, [haiga] are not much in little, but enough in little. It is in haiga that we see most clearly, directly and instantaneously the nature of haiku, its willing limitations; its 'sensationism'; its unsentimental love of nature; its lack of *iki*, elegance; its appreciation of imperfection; its skilful unskilfulness; its 'blessed are the poor'; its combination of the poetic vague and the poetic definite; its human warmth; its avoidance of violence and terror; its dislike of holiness; its turning a blind eye to grandeur and majesty; its unobtrusive good taste; its still, small voice.

[1] *The cover design incorporates a sketch of a toad which is part of a Japanese haiga from the eighteenth century.*

13

THE HUMOUR OF SENRYU

(The main part of this Section is Chapter 18 of 'Japanese Life and Character in Senryu'. In the Introduction to this book, Blyth says:)

The fundamental thing in the Japanese character is a peculiar combination of poetry and humour, using both words in a wide and profound yet specific sense. 'Poetry' means the ability to see, to know by intuition what is interesting, what is really valuable in things and persons. More exactly, it is the creating of interest, of value. 'Humour' means joyful, unsentimental pathos that arises from the paradox inherent in the nature of things. Poetry and humour are thus very close; we may say that they are two different aspects of the same thing. Poetry is *satori* [1]; it is seeing all things as good. Humour is laughing at all things; in Buddhist parlance, seeing that 'all things are empty in their self-nature', and rejoicing in this truth.

(On p. 209 of the same book he says:)

Haiku have little to do with science or philosophy or psychology. They are unaffected by the theories and discoveries of Darwin and Plato and Freud. Senryu, however, are apparently factual, have a certain philosophy of life in them, and as for psychology, senryu, like Cassius, 'look quite through the deeds of men'. Nevertheless, senryu are not mere records of psychological situations and comical analyses of human weakness. They are of course full of psychology, but with something which transcends while including it. A really good senryu has what is called in Japanese literary criticism 'after-taste', *atoaji*, what remains, to change the metaphor, echoing in the mind 'long after it is heard no more.'

The point of all this is that [ ] what is really good in it is not the psychology which it is full of, but the poetry, which comes and goes in some mysterious but indubitable way.

> *Oshienai koto o shitteru teinôji*
> The weak-minded child;
> He knows
> What he was not taught.   *Hyôraku*

This is true, and equally true, of all of us. What we really know is what we have picked out of our experiences [ ].

(Now to Chapter 18.)

[1] *See page 28*

Rather than give a solemn and unhumorous account of the origins and nature of humour, it may be better to illustrate the various kinds of humour in senryu, [—grim humour, tragic humour, irony, linguistic humour, kindly humour, Shakespearean humour, humour of exposed pretence, humour of indirectness, humour of stupidity, and parody.]

1. Grim Humour

> *Suppari to naorimashita to hana ga ochi*
> Quite recovered,
> But his nose
> Has fallen off.

In this sort of senryu, the humour needs to be strong enough to prevent the verse from falling into cruelty, and the reader of course must play his part in this. In the next example, it is the sentiment which must not be allowed to dominate the verse. Grimness must be added to prevent the pathos from killing the humour:

> *Ima suteru ko ni aritake no chi o nomase*
> Going to desert her child,
> She gives it
> All the milk she has.

The mother is going to leave her baby to be picked up by someone, and will never see it again. She is deserting it, leaving it to its fate, but gives it all the milk she has in her body. There is a contradiction here which belongs to every region of human life. [   ]

> *Nyôbô e muketa shisen e teishu muki*
> Against the eyes upon his wife
> The husband turns
> *His* eyes.

Someone is staring at his wife, and the husband glares at the man to show him who he is. The point lies in the force of will, instead of physical strength, which is exerted one against the other.

2. Tragic Humour

The following senryu is a particularly fine example of tragedy and humour united.

Yoshiwara e muite Ueno de kubi o tsuri
He hanged himself
At Ueno,
Facing the Yoshiwara.

The violence of tragicomedy here is Hogarthian. To commit suicide is a terrible and ghastly thing, but to do it because of some wretched prostitute is a kind of parody. But the parody also disinfects the scene of all falsity, eternal love, and other sentimentality. We see a human being stripped bare of all but his painful life and solitary death. There is also another element, seen in the place, Ueno, of exhibitionism, a quality of which the greatest men are not free.

3. Irony

Itoko nimo shiro yô kuru to tabi no rusu
He may be her cousin, of course,
But he comes *very* often
When the master's away on a journey.

[   ] It is very hard to make a tactful reply to this remark.

Unconscious irony is a favourite form of humour with senryu writers, for we get the pleasure of contrast in both the irony itself and in the obliviousness of the person concerned:

Yoku shimete nero to ii-ii nusumi ni de
'Shut up the house carefully
Before you go to bed,'
He repeats, going off to burgle.

The point of this senryu lies in the sublime unconsciousness of the thief that he is one. He is a private citizen as far as his own house is concerned. Sometimes it is the irony of fate that senryu displays to us.

Horerareta koto ato de shiru gojûnen
Knowing she was mad on me
Fifty years
Afterwards.   *Kenkabô*

The impotence of man with regard to time is keenly felt here. Being told, or suddenly realizing, that a certain person is in love with us is a great pleasure and source of satisfaction, but to do so fifty years after the event brings mixed feelings and a kind of melancholy, mild cynicism which belongs especially to senryu.

123

Kanemochi o mikubitte yuku hatsu-gatsuo
The first bonito;
It passes by,
Despising the rich.

In all times and places the poor have thought more of their stomachs. The rich are rich because they have loved money and power more than the pleasure of the moment. But the senryu writer has perceived this sociological fact poetically. The bonitos go swinging by in the baskets hanging from the shoulder-pole, and their eyes seem to disdain the rich people who want to taste them but will not pay the money.

Mamagoto no sembei chisaku chisaku wari
She divides up the wafer
For those playing at housekeeping,
Ever so, ever so small.   *Monsen*

This shows the inherent meanness of mankind, and of women especially, that the little girl, who takes the part of the mother of the house, should divide up the biscuit into such tiny pieces.

Oriru toki seki o yuzutta jinkakusha
What a beautiful character!
He gives up his seat to someone,—
When he gets off.   *Ryûsei*

The car is full, and in front of him there stands, for quite a time, a woman with a baby. Suddenly, he stands up and in a very gentlemanly way offers her his seat, graciously receiving the profuse thanks,— but he is getting out! So many senryu deal with just those things which intellectual polite society does not admit. This has been pointed out by Aldous Huxley, but too cynically and misanthropically. Senryu deals with such matters more lightly.

Ryôhô ni hige no haeteru neko no koi
Both of them
With whiskers,
Loves of the cats.

It is very odd, when one thinks of it, that both the cats have whiskers. It makes the whole affair seem homosexual. And yet the word 'heterosexual', which we must apply to human beings, does not sound any too good either.

4. Linguistic Humour

> *Kokû o tsukami sorikaeri nagai hi da*
> Gripping the empty air,
> He throws back his head,
> 'What an interminable day!'

The chief merit of this verse is the first two lines, which well express the attitude of a man yawning. The first line illustrates one of the special characteristics of senryu, a figurative description of ordinary actions, but taking these descriptions literally. Another example:

> *Muko-erabi suru uchi yanagi usu ni nari*
> While her partner in life
> Is being chosen,
> The willow tree becomes a mortar.

As a woman becomes older she gets broad in the beam. What is interesting is the way in which the girth registers the years, just like the rings of a tree.

> *Sui musuko karai oyaji ni amai haha*
> Sour son,
> Peppery father,
> Sweet mother.

These epithets are clever and true to life, that is, Japanese life.

> *Asagao wa asane no hito ni shigamitsura*
> To the late riser,
> The morning-glory
> Makes a wry face.

The *asagao* is literally the 'morning-face'. By the time the lie-abed has arisen, the flowers are wilting, and present a fading, wrinkled, scornful, reproving face.

5. Kindly Humour

There is a certain amiable, benevolent humour in senryu, which is nevertheless not allowed to fall into kindness. It has no malice, but a certain tolerant contempt mingled with its affection. For example:

> *Hanami sa to gejo karuishi de te o migaki*
> 'We're going cherry-blossom viewing!'

Replies the servant,
Scrubbing her hands with pumice.

There is a discord here between the servant's great dirty hands, and the delicate pink blossoms, but also there is some secret harmony between them and her spirit. This is also what we feel in Katherine Mansfield's *At the Bay*, when the servant goes out for the day. Theoretically, a person with big red chapped hands should not be able to enjoy the delicate beauty of the cherry blossoms, but. . . There is always a 'but'. Perhaps the 'but' is the poetry.

> *Berabô ni umai to homeru zatsu na kyaku*
> 'Thundering good!'
> Praises
> The uncouth visitor.

This senryu is very delicate. It points to the state of mind of a man who is praised for something or other by a visitor who is at the same time so rough and ready that the praise seems almost cancelled by the rude manner in which it is expressed. *Berabô* means a blockhead, and *berabô ni*, awfully, exceedingly. It is as if one should say to a parson, 'Hellishly good!' or smack a very dignified gentleman on the back.

> *Kuru hito wo mushi ga shirasuru kusa no io*
> The insects tell
> That someone is coming:
> The grassy hut.

This senryu de-poeticises the poetic life. The insects that serenade the hermit and afford him a subject for his poetical effusions, are also a sort of buzzer in reverse, announcing visitors and others by their sudden silence.
[   ]

> *Waga seko ga kubeki yoi nari shichi o oki*
> It is the evening
> My beloved should come,
> Having pawned something.

This is based on a waka in the *Kokinshû* by Sotôri Hime who was the mistress of the Emperor:

Wago seko ga kubeki yoi nari sasagani no
kumo no furumai kanete shirushi mo
It is an evening
My beloved should come,
For the spider
Has been at its work,
Foretelling this.

It was believed that a spider making its web in the evening was a sign of the coming of one's love. In the senryu the woman is of course a courtesan, and her lover must pawn something to get some money for her.

Tsurenu yatsu biku o nozoku to kakusu nari
Having caught nothing,
He hides the creel,
When someone wants to peep in.

Either to hide the fish basket, or smile a sheepish, fishy smile, —is there any other alternative?

6. Shakespearean Humour

The humour of Shakespeare is a peculiar combination of all kinds of qualities; wit, brevity, indirectness, humanity, forgiveness, understanding, inevitability. It is seen most vividly and significantly in Falstaff, and here is a senryu that he would have enjoyed.

Attesae iwanya goke ni oite oya
Sometimes when it's a wife,—
How much more so
In the case of a widow!

Even a wife may slip from the path of virtue. For a widow it is easier and more understandable.

7. Humour of Exposed Pretence

There is a universal desire to explode the bubbles, to break through the camouflage, to tear off the masks by which human beings hide their true selves. The odd thing is that the more we try to prevent others from knowing our true self, the more we reveal, for in life as in art, to hide is to show.

Unubore o yameraba hoka ni hore-te nashi
When he stops

Being in love with himself,
Who will love him?

This senryu does not imply that self-love prevents others from loving him, but that, as the comic song says, 'Everybody's loved by some-oooone', at least by himself. But this is just *why* he fancies himself. Good, true, and beautiful people are admired, so there is no need for them to love themselves. In other words, there is no virtue whatever in humility or altruism or selflessness. Somebody must love us; it is only a question who, other people or ourselves. This is the profound philosophy of senryu, that goes beyond Thomas Aquinas or Någårjuna.

> *Daimyaku kotaete shisei wa ten ni ari*
> The Assistant Doctor replies,
> 'Life and death
> Depend on the Will of Heaven.'

The Assistant parrots the words of Confucius, just as he reels off the words of the Chinese book of medicine, *Pentsao Kangmu*, by Li Shi-chen, 1578:

> *Honzô no tôri daimyaku shaberu nari*
> The Assistant Doctor
> Chatters
> According to the Materia Medica.

> *Aisatsu ga sumu to tsumetai me ni kaeri*
> After the greetings are over,
> He becomes
> Cold-eyed again.   *Tôkan*

This verse reminds us how much stronger manners are than morality.

> *Oshakasama umareochiru to miso o age*
> When Buddha was born
> He immediately
> Blew his own trumpet.

It is said that Såkyamuni cried, on being born, 'Above and below the heavens, I only am the Holy One'. This singing his own praises seems out of keeping with the Buddhist virtue of humility.

8. Humour of Indirectness

Mere indirectness has something comical in it. The reason for this must be in the revelation of the disparity of cause and effect, ideal and real, silence and speech.

> *Shikarazu ni tonari no yome o homete oki*
> Not a word of blame,—
> But praising
> The bride next door.

Praise is always blame of someone else, or the same person some other time, and obviously so when a mother-in-law praises another bride. Another example, more acid:

> *Towa shirazu sazo rusuchû wa osewasama*
> Knowing nothing about it,
> 'Many thanks for your kindness
> While I was away.'

'It' means the relation between the man he is thanking and his own wife. The obliquity and obscurity of the verse represents life flowing on, regardless of those details which at times seem so important.

9. The Humour of Stupidity

Much laughter is caused by, or reveals, a sense of superiority over the folly or weakness of others; for example:

> *Naidan no hibachi futari de ijiri-keshi*
> In a tête-à-tête over the brazier,
> They both fidgeted with the fire,
> And put it out.

Two people, engrossed in private talk, keep playing with the coals without thinking of what they are doing, and it goes out. We have also a contrast here between the lofty concentration, on something else, of the two human beings; and the independence of things, which will not allow themselves to be mistreated or abused, but will rather go out of existence than be treated with indignity.

> *Yubi sashite zatô ni oshie warawareru*
> Pointing the way
> To a blind shampooer,
> Gets us laughed at.

This does not seem to be very amusing, until we see a man bowing and gesticulating at the telephone.

> *Tsuru yatsu mo tsuru yatsu miru yatsu mo yatsu*
> The creatures angling!
> The creatures looking at the creatures angling!
> What creatures they are!

This is amusing in the original from its fourfold repetition of *yatsu*, 'chap' or 'fellow'. It gives one a feeling of the 'many-headed multitudes', so small in the head.

> *Echigo-ya ga miesô na mono to Fuji de ii*
> 'Echigoya should be visible
> From here, surely,'
> They say from Mount Fuji.

'Echigoya' was the name of the most famous draper's shop in Edo. Mount Fuji could be seen easily from here and the mountain and the shop stood in a certain peculiar relation of richness and grandeur to the people of Edo. Some people climbed up the mountain and expected to see Echigoya from there, because Mount Fuji was visible from Echigoya, and they were incredulous when they found it impossible to place it.   [   ]

> *Mizu o yobu sanyaku oshi no yô ni ii*
> The medicine powder;
> Calling for water
> As if he were dumb.   *Dokushimbô*

A man puts the powder in his mouth, and then thinks of the water. He calls for it in dumb show. Besides the humour of this, or through it, we feel the pathos of human nature, so upset by a little powder in the mouth.

10. Parody

> *Korobazuba okina no yukimi hate ga nashi*
> If the old chap
> Does not tumble down
> There's no end to his snow-viewing.

This is a very good example of senryu as parody, taking literally the poetical hyperbole of Bashô's well-known verse in which he expresses his love of the beauty of the snow and snow-scenery.

> *Iza saraba yukimi ni korobu tokoro made*
> Now then!
> Let's go snow-viewing
> Till we tumble down!

> *Waga mono to omoeba karushi ô-zutsumi*
> When I think it is mine, —
> How light it is,
> This big parcel!   *Suigetsubô*

This comes from the well-known haiku of Kikaku, which is itself practically a senryu:

> *Waga mono to omoeba karushi kasa no yuki*
> When I think it is mine,
> How light it is,
> The snow on my *kasa*!

Suigetsubô's verse asserts the psychological principle of self-interest, as it affects our judgement and effusion of vital energy. But the historical association and historical flavour give it some slight poetical value.

> *Shôjiki no kôbe jûgatsu karû nari*
> The head of the honest man
> Becomes light
> In [November].

[November] is also called Kannazuki, 'the God-absent month', for in that month the gods all over Japan gathered at Izumo to discuss what had occurred during the past year, and what would happen in the coming year. There is also a Japanese proverb:

God lodges in an honest man's head.

The senryu has combined these two ideas. The honest man's head is always heavy except in [November]. We should note the extraordinary ingeniousness of this verse, and its cynicism, which will allow no proverb or custom or superstition to pass unscathed.   [   ]

Zashiki-rô yume wa kuruwa o kake-meguri
House-imprisoned,
My dreams hover
Over a prostitute quarter.

This is a blasphemous and excellent parody of Bashô's death-verse:

Tabi ni yande yume wa kareno o kake-meguru
Ill on a journey,
My dreams hover
Over a withered moor.

Araumi ya yami o kite neru gakuya-mono
The green-room men
Sleep, covering themselves
With the raging sea and the darkness.

On the *Kabuki* stage night is shown by a black curtain hanging from the ceiling. The sea is represented by a blue cloth plaited here and there, on the floor. *Araumi ya* is probably taken from Bashô's famous haiku, but here *ya* is not an exclamation; it means 'and'.

Dôgu-kata iwa o chigitte hana o kami
The stage carpenter
Tears off the rock,
And blows his nose.

The rock on the stage is made of paper. We have here a sudden vision of the magical nature of matter.

Hitodama de zôri o sagasu gakuya-ban
The green-room man
Looks for his sandals
With the ghost-fire.

On the stage the ghost of a dead person is represented by a waving will-o'-the-wisp-like torch. It is used here for a very humble purpose. [ ]

(about the intensive practice of Zazen) 'I think it very good for a time, but ..... I feel inclined to warn you against a humourless Zen. The secret of life consists in being always and never serious.'
(from a letter Blyth wrote to James W. Hackett, 1 April 1962)

(about haiku in education) ....haiku should be the chief subject in primary and secondary schools in every country in the world. But it should be prohibited in the universities, and on no account should children ever be examined on them, or forced to explain them. How about my own explanations? Some say they are better than many of the original haiku. Some say they should be omitted. I myself agree with both views.

('History of Haiku', Vol.2.)

14

HAIKU IN MODERN TIMES — REVOLUTION OR DECLINE?

(This extract is from 'History of Haiku', Vol.2.)

[   ] Shiki is said to have revolutionized haiku. He endeavoured to enable people to write without any very definite spiritual or religious background; to write haiku though not walking in the Way of Haiku. This Way of Haiku, as originated by Bashô two hundred years before (Shiki died in 1902, Bashô in 1694) was a way of poverty. It involved a pantheistic view of life, though the haiku were not intellectual; it was mystical, yet the oneness of things, and the unity of the poet with them was never expressed directly. The Japanese have always felt, rightly enough, that poetry must not be philosophical or religious, but they have never realized that they were unconsciously resting on the paradoxical, non-egoistic, universal, democratic basis of Mahayana Buddhism. The influence of the West was towards the weakening of this basis, formally and spiritually. We do not feel it implicit in the haiku of Shiki, as we do even in Buson, to whom Shiki turned rather than to Bashô and Issa. We may say then that Shiki was both the product of and the hastener of this tendency, a world-tendency indeed, towards irreligion, unpoeticalness, and mechanization.

Another and more subtle way in which Shiki helped in the decadence of haiku was by his dropping of renga[1], which had continued for seven or eight hundred years. This perhaps is the chief reason for the decline of haiku since 1900. Man is a social animal, and haikai was a social poetry. It linked poetical minds together, and the hokku was simply the beginning of this chain. The hokku became haiku and had no further purpose, no object of stimulating a train of poetical thought, it was isolated and unnatural, that is, unsocial and unsociable. In this sense, Shiki gave the *coup de grace* to haiku by declaring that renga was not literature.

Bashô, Buson, and Issa were teachers and masters of renga, the linked poems from which haiku developed, or rather, from which it detached itself. Renga were the continuum, of which haiku were the isolated phrases and themes. When the actual or implied nexus of renga was gone, haiku found themselves beating their ineffectual wings in the void. This is, in my opinion, their present lamentable condition, and until haiku are once more linked up

---

[1] *renga: a chain of verses, usually composed by a group of poets, alternately 5-7-5 and 7-7. The first verse (hokku) was provided by a master; typically so excellent that it could stand alone; and out of this haiku was born.*

again with visible and invisible ties, they will continue to be thin, rootless, unechoing, immemorable, just little gasps of what should be a steady and unbroken breathing.

Shiki began with his *shasei-ron*, the theory of the delineation of nature, but he soon found that he had also to include the delineation of his own mind. A hundred percent objectivity is not possible, even to a scientist, who also sees things according to the construction of his own mind, not to speak of his body. Shiki however makes a mistake, at least of terminology, when he writes in *Haiku Taiyô*:

> Haiku is a part of literature. Literature is part of art (*bijutsu*). For this reason, the standard of literature is the standard of beauty.

Haiku is not really literature, for it dispenses with words as far as possible. But even in ordinary literature, beauty is not the standard. (Keats made the same mistake.) Haiku does not aim at beauty any more than does the music of Bach. The universe does not aim at beauty. Beauty is a by-product; it is a means, as Darwin showed us; it is never an end. Shiki's conclusion, however, is correct:

> Painting, sculpture, music, drama, poetry, novels are all to be judged by the same standard.

But this standard is not beauty, however inexplicable and indefinable beauty may be. It is poetry, to which beauty is friend and companion, but not a married partner. Bashô perhaps knew this; Buson, an artist, did not, neither did Shiki, his follower. The history of haiku would have been different if only Buson and Shiki had realised, as Issa did, that it is the nature of humanity and the humanity of nature which is the important thing, not the beauty or the harmony. Haiku should always have been what Wordsworth calls 'seeing into the life of things'. Buson was an artist; Shiki was a sick man; and what Thoreau calls 'the health of nature' was not their chief concern. [ ]

15

WORLD HAIKU

(This chapter, the final one in 'History of Haiku', Vol. 2, is the last Blyth ever published. With hindsight, it may seem sketchy; but we must remember that, in 1964, the English-speaking 'haiku movement' was still in its infancy. Much of its initial impetus was, in fact, due to Blyth, as well as to Harold G. Henderson. Apart from his books, which were attracting a following, especially in North America, Blyth's correspondence with poets and scholars had a significant part to play. Among these correspondents, from 1958 to 1964, was the young American, J.W. Hackett, who was beginning to break new ground as a haiku poet.

Prior to their eventual publication, Hackett sent Blyth a number of his haiku for comment, and Blyth was assiduously critical in a most positive way. He even sought to find a publisher for Hackett's poetry; and inserted 30 of Hackett's haiku, not without the odd word of criticism, in this 'World Haiku' chapter. 'I want to show people, I mean Japanese people', he wrote to Hackett in a letter, 'that there are Americans who can outdo them in their own field. Or to put it another way, I would like to get rid of nationalism in culture, as well as in other things.'

We have omitted most of the thirty Hackett poems here, partly to keep the focus on Blyth, but also because the versions which Hackett eventually presented to the public are often different from those which appeared in 'History of Haiku'.)

The latest development in the history of haiku is one which nobody foresaw,—the writing of haiku outside Japan, not in the Japanese language. We may now assert with some confidence that the day is coming when haiku will be written in Russia (though communistic haiku, like capitalistic or Christian or Buddhist or atheistic haiku, is a glorious impossibility), in the Celebes, in Sardinia. What a pleasing prospect, what an Earthly Paradise it will be, the Esquimaux blowing on their fingers as they write haiku about the sun that never sets or rises, the pygmies composing jungle haiku on the gorilla and the python, the nomads of the Sahara and Gobi deserts seeing a grain of sand in a world!

But wherever haiku are composed, the problem of the form must arise. Europeans and Americans have to decide whether their haiku are to be in rhyming couplets or triplets, alliterative verse, free verse, what some rude people call 'a dribble of prose', or in five, seven, five syllables as in Japanese. As far as the last is concerned, a strict adherence to 5, 7, 5 syllables in English has produced some odd translations of Japanese haiku. For example,[ ] the following appeared in No. VII of a Monograph Committee, Los Angeles, 1964:

> Old pond, ancient pool:
> A frog jumping plunges in:
> Waterish splash-splosh.

This is 5, 7, 5, but the last line suggests that Bashô himself fell in, and (as was probably actually the case) could not swim. Even the first line, in order to get five syllables, repeats itself, and then is too short, giving the impression of the vocative. A translation of another famous verse:

> Bare barren branch on
> Which a crow has alighted: autumn
> Nightfall darkening.

This is a line of 17 syllables, sliced arbitrarily into 5, 7, 5. The fact is that 'syllables' does not have the same meaning for the Japanese, the Romans and Greeks, and the English. For us, 'a' is a syllable, 'clothes' is a syllable. To push the matter to the extreme, take the following:

> In a potato
> Those groans whose forced prayers change nought
> Can never occur.

This is 5, 7, 5, but to eye and ear, and to the sense of counting, the 5, 7, 5 has no meaning whatever.

The philosophic significance of 5, 7, 5, in Japanese syllables, may be this. Seventeen such syllables are one emission of breath, one exhalation of soul. The division into three gives us the feeling of ascent, attainment, and resolution of experience. Five, five, is symmetry; five seven, and seven five, are asymmetry, double that of symmetry, which is proper in our geometrical but fortuitous universe.[1] **The haiku form is thus a simple and yet deeply 'natural' form, compared to the sonnet, blank verse, and other borrowed forms of verse in English. The ideal, that is, the occasionally attainable haiku form in English, would perhaps be three short lines, the second a little longer than the other two; a two-three-two rhythm, but not regularly iambic or anapaestic; rhyme avoided, even if felicitous and accidental. A season word is not necessary, nor even a season, but is greatly advantageous, as suggesting one quarter of the year in time.**

[1]*Consider the rmathematical proportions which are unique to 5-7-5 : 7 is 140% of 5, and 10 (5+5) is 143% of 7. There is a sort of reversing balance.*

The following thirty verses are chosen, not altogether at random, from a forthcoming book of haiku by J. W. Hackett of San Francisco. They are in no way mere imitations of Japanese haiku, nor literary diversions. They are (aimed at) the Zen experience, the realising, the making real in oneself of the thing-in-itself, impossible to rational thought, but possible, 'all poets believe', in experience. Mr Hackett himself writes, in a letter:

> I regard 'haiku' as *fundamentally* existential, rather than literary. Or if you will, as primarily an experience, rather than a form of poetry. Bashô's statement that: 'Haiku is simply what is happening in this place, at this moment', shows that he regarded intuitive experience to be the *basis* of haiku. And Now, his criterion, is my own.

> If this haiku experience can be expressed in 17 syllables (or even 5-7-5) without padding or syntactical contrivance, all well and good. If not, then the experience should be rendered freely, in the manner best serving its comprehension and effect. The Japanese masters strayed from 5-7-5, as do many modern Japanese poets. Certainly, the poet writing in English is entitled to the same licence, and more...I use 2 lines whenever I wish and there is no doubt that some haiku experiences can be more naturally expressed in this way. It seems clear that the whole matter of syllables and lines is an arbitrary one, and should be. For haiku is ultimately more than a form (or even a kind) of poetry: it is a Way—one of living awareness. Haiku's real treasure is its touchstone of the present. This, together with its rendering of the Suchness of things, gives haiku a supra-literary mission, one of moment.

(Here followed the 30 haiku by James W. Hackett. We give just two; in each instance on the left, the version quoted by Blyth, and on the right, the version published later by Hackett.)

Bitter morning:	A bitter morning:
Sparrows sitting	sparrows sitting together
Without necks.	without any necks.
Chopping a knotty block ...	Chopping kindling from
In every stick of kindling	a knotty block...in each stick
Part of its shape.	a part of its shape.

In these excellent verses, occasionally there is sensation only; more often there is too much ostensive, that is, overt thought. The problem for haiku in any language, as for life itself in any age, is how to put thought completely into sensation, how to make sensation thought-full. In addition,—and this has only too often been forgotten by the Japanese haiku poets themselves,—sensation must be intense, though not violent, the thinking all-inclusive and subtle, not parochial and complicated. But after all, which, is more important, to write (haiku) or to live? Thoreau answers:

> My life has been the poem I would have writ,
> But I could not both live and utter it.

Which is more important, to love a particular animal, and all of them, or to understand Zen? If we answer that they are the same thing, this is true, though how many people in the world know even this? But it is much more true, it is more Zen to answer, 'To love a particular animal'. It is this which makes a life an unwritten poem. Writing haiku, and the desire for (more and more) enlightenment is the last infirmity of noble mind. We must not write haiku, we must not write, we must not live, to fulfil ourselves, or to share our experiences with others. We must not aim at immortality or even timelessness; we must not aim. Infinity and eternity come of themselves or not at all. 'God first loved us'. Wordsworth once more:

> Think you, of all this mighty sum
> Of things forever speaking,
> That nothing of itself will come,
> But we must still be seeking?

[ ] every day that passes seems to make the appreciation of poetry a more rare thing. Japan and America and Russia are all alike, looking only for the sensational, the scientific, the safe, the silly.

(Thirty years on, would he have added 'the sordid' and 'the accountable'?)

But I think anyway that if I had remained in England I could not have had any of my books published.
(from a letter Blyth wrote to James W. Hackett, October 1962.)

The aim of senryu is to bring out into the open the sentimentality, affectation, swindling, and hypocrisy in the world; to expose the unobserved or purposely overlooked contradictions in what men say and what they actually do; to lay bare all the hidden motives, the secret shame, the useless wisdom, and foolish misery of mankind.

('Japanese Life and Character in Senryu'.)

BIBLIOGRAPHY OF THE PUBLISHED WORKS OF R H BLYTH RELEVANT TO THE CONTENTS OF THIS ANTHOLOGY

1 ZEN IN ENGLISH LITERATURE AND ORIENTAL CLASSICS (Hokuseido, 1942, and Dutton paperback edn.1960) 5pp preface + 435 pp. + index. Chapter headings as follows: 1 What is Zen? 2 Religion is Poetry 3 Poetry is Every-day Life 4 Directness is All 5 Subjective and Objective 6 Concrete and Abstract 7 The Unregarded River of Our Life 8 Everything Depends on the Mind 9 The Mind of Man 10 Words, Words, Words 11 Figures of Speech 12 The Pale Cast of Thought 13 Paradox 14 Don Quixote 15 Pantheism, Mysticism, Zen-I 16 Pantheism, Mysticism, Zen - II 17 'Religious' Poetry 18 Non-Attachment - I 19 Non-Attachment - II 20 Non-Attachment - III 21 Non-Attachment - IV 22 Death 23 Children 24 Idiots and Old Men 25 Poverty 26 Animals 27 Wordsworth 28 Shakespeare.

2 HAIKU (in 4 vols.) (Hokuseido, 1949-52) VOLUME ONE: EASTERN CULTURE (1949) 14pp preface + 393 pp. + appendices and index. Chapter headings as follows: (Section 1 - The Spiritual Origins of Haiku) 1 Buddhism 2 Zen/ Bashô and Zen 3 Taoism 4 Chinese Poetry 5 Confucianism 6 Oriental Art 7 Waka 8 Renku 9 Nô, Ikebana, Cha no Yu 10 Shintô (Section 2 - Zen, the State of Mind for Haiku) 1 Selflessness 2 Loneliness 3 Grateful Acceptance 4 Wordlessness 5 Non-Intellectuality 6 Contradiction 7 Humour 8 Freedom 9 Non-Morality 10 Simplicity 11 Materiality 12 Love 13 Courage (Section 3 - Haiku and Poetry) 1 Haiku and Poetry 2 Haiku in English Poetry 3 Poetry (Section 4 - The Four Great Haiku Poets) 1 Bashô 2 Buson 3 Issa 4 Shiki (Section 5 -The Technique of Haiku) 1 Humour and Puns 2 Brevity 3 The Japanese Language 4 Onomatopoeia 6 The Form of Haiku 6 Kireji 7 Haiku Sequences 8 The Seasons 9 Translation.

VOLUME TWO: SPRING (1950) 5pp preface + 382 pp. Sections as follows: 1 The New Year 2 Spring: the Season 3 Spring: Sky and Elements 4 Spring: Fields and Mountains 5 Spring: Gods and Buddhas 6 Spring: Human Affairs 7 Spring: Birds and Beasts 8 Spring: Trees and Flowers.

VOLUME THREE: SUMMER AND AUTUMN (1952) 6pp preface + 442 pp. Sections as follows: 1 Summer: the Season 2 Summer: Sky and Elements 3 Summer: Fields and Mountains 4 Summer: Gods and Buddhas 5 Summer: Human Affairs 6 Summer: Birds and Beasts 7 Summer: Trees and Flowers 8 Autumn: The Season 9 Autumn: Sky and Elements.

VOLUME FOUR: AUTUMN AND WINTER (1952) 36pp preface + 366pp + appendices and index. Sections as follows: 1 Autumn: Fields and Mountains 2 Autumn: Gods and Buddhas 3 Autumn: Human Affairs 4 Autumn: Birds and Beasts 5 Autumn: Trees and Flowers 6 Winter: the Season 7 Winter: Sky and Elements 8 Winter: Fields and Mountains 9 Winter: Gods and Buddhas 10 Winter: Human Affairs 11 Winter: Birds and Beasts 12 Winter: Trees and Flowers.

3 SENRYU—JAPANESE SATYRICAL VERSES (Hokuseido, 1949) 2pp preface + 230pp. Sections and headings as follows:
Introduction. (Section 1: Haiku and Senryu) 1 Nature and Man 2 All and One 3 Simple and Complex 4 Religious and Irreligious 5 Romantic and Realistic 6 Poetry and Parody 7 Tender and Tough 8 Emotion and Intellect 9 Delicacy 10 Half-said and All-said 11 Humour 12 Transcendence 13 Democracy 14 Sex 15 Zen 16 Religion 17 Is Senryu Poetry? (Section 2: The Origins and Technique of Senryu) 1 Vocabulary and Syntax 2 Poetic Brevity 3 Personification 4 Colloquialisms 5 The Composition of Senryu & Customs and Manners 7 Proscripts 8 Anonymity 9 Principle of Selection 10 Conclusion. (Section 3 Senryu about) 1 Women 2 Children 3 Mothers 4 Fathers 5 Wives 6 Husbands 7 Mothers-in-Law 8 Other Relations 9 Professions 10 Animals 11 Things 12 Historical 13 Psychology 14 Pictures of Life.

4 BUDDHIST SERMONS ON CHRISTIAN TEXTS (Kokudosha, 1952) 4pp introduction + 93pp. In two sections: 1 Sermons 2 Parallel Passages from the Christian Mystics and Zen Writings.

5 JAPANESE HUMOUR (Japan Tourist Bureau, 1957) 12pp preface + 184pp.

6 ORIENTAL HUMOUR (Hokuseido, 1959) 2pp preface + 567pp + bibliography + index. Introduction and 3 parts, with headings as follows: (Part 1 - China) 1 Chinese Humour 2 The Chinese Classics 3 Chinese Poetry 4 Ghost Stories 5 Liehtse 6 Proverbs 7 Taoism 8 Zen 9 Short Stories, to the Ch'ing Period 10 Short Stories, from 1643 (Part 2 - Korea) 1 Korean Humour - Proverbs 2 Korean Short Stories (Part 3 - Japan) 1 Japanese Humour 2 Chinese Influence on Japan 3 Japanese Literature - I 4 Japanese Literature - II 5 The History of Japanese Caricature 6 Japanese Proverbs 7 Yanagidaru - I 8 Yanagidaru - II 9 Yanagidaru - III 10 Other Old Senryu 11 Modern Senryu 12 Ghost Stories 13 Short Stories - I (up to 1750) 14 Short Stories - II (after 1750) 15 Epilogue and Chronological Chart of Japanese Humour.

7 JAPANESE LIFE AND CHARACTER IN SENRYU (Hokuseido, 1961) 2pp preface + 628pp + bibliography + index. Introduction and 5 parts. (Part 1 - Chronological Survey of Senryu) 1 General Outline of Senryu from Genroku to Meiji 2 Genroku to Hôreki 1688-1764 - I 3 Genroku to Hôreki 1688-1764 - II 4 Meiwa 1764-1771 5 Anei 1772-1780 6 Temmei 1781-1789 7 Kansei 1789-1801 8 Kyôwa 1801-1804 and Bunka 1804-1818 9 Bunsei 1818-1830 10 Tempô 1830-1844 11 Meiji 1868-1911 12 Taishô 1912-1925 13 Shôwa 1926- (Part 2 - Senryu) 1 Psychology 2 Women 3 Animals 4 Unconsidered Trifles 5 The Humour of Senryu 6 Professions 7 Historical Senryu 8 Domestic and Daily Life 9 Buddhism 10 The Poetry of Senryu 11 Scenes of This Fleeting World 12 The Philosophy of Senryu (Part 3 - A Year of Senryu) 1 Spring 2 Summer 3 Autumn 4 Winter (Part 4 - The Meiji Senryu Poets) 1 Inoue Kenkabô 2 Saikai Kuraki (Part 5 - Epilogue).

8 ZEN AND ZEN CLASSICS (in 5 vols.) (Hokuseido, 1960-70) VOLUME ONE - FROM THE UPANISHADS TO HUINENG (1960) 1p preface + 113pp + bibliography. Chapter headings as follows: 1 What is Zen? 2 The History of Zen (from 1000 B.C. to 715 A.D.) 3 The Believing Mind (the Hsinhsinming) 4 Song of the Way (the Chengtaoke) 5 The Platform Sutra 6 Epilogue. VOLUME TWO-HISTORY OF ZEN, 713-867 A.D.(1964) 4pp preface + 204 pp + index. Chapter headings as follows: 1 The Five Sects 2 Gozu Zen and Rôan Zen 3 Enô and his Disciples 4 Sekitô's Disciples - I 5 Sekitô's Disciples - II 6 Seppô 7 Seppô's Disciples - I 8 Seppô's Disciples - II 9 Hôgen 10 Hôgen's Disciples 11 Yakusan to Sekisô 12 Sensu, Kassan, Shôzan 13 Tôzan 14 Sôzan and Ungo 15 Unmon - I 16 Unmon - I I 17 Unmon - I I I 18 The Sandôkai 13 The Hôkyôzammai 20 The Poems of Hanshan - I 21 The Poems of Hanshan - II 22 Zen, Mysticism, Existentialism 23 Ways and the Way 24 Nature, Human Nature, the Buddha Nature, the Poetic Nature 25 Defects of Zen 26 Epilogue. VOLUME THREE -HISTORY OF ZEN, 867-1260 A.D. (NANGAKU BRANCH) (1970) 2pp preface + 185pp. Chapter headings as follows; 1 The Disciples of Tôzan 2 Nangaku and Baso 3 Nansen and Jôshû 4 Hyakujô and his Disciples 5 Obaku and his Disciples 6 Rinzai and his Disciples. VOLUME FOUR - MUMONKAN (1966) 5pp preface + 326 pp + index. Chapter headings as follows: 1 Introduction 2 Cases I - XLVIII 3 Mumon's Postscript 4 Mumon's Warnings 5 Sôju's Verse on Oryû's Three Barriers 6 Môkyô's Epilogue 7 Amban's Forty-ninth Case 8 Postscript. VOLUME FIVE - TWENTY-FIVE ZEN ESSAYS (1962) 4pp preface + 210pp + index. Chapter headings as follows: 1 Zen, Christianity, and Buddhism 2 Zen and Culture 3 Zen and Humour 4 Zen and Reason 5 Zen and Society 6 Zen, Sex and Love 7 Zen and Poetry-I 8 Zen and Poetry-II 9 Zen and Poetry-III 10 Zen and Shelley 11 Zen and Grammar 12 Zen and Women 13 Zen in European Art 14 Zen and Music 15 Zen and Japan 16 Zen and Nô 17 Zen and Zen 18 The History of Zen in the West 19 Four Japanese Zen Monks: Ryokan, Ikkyû, Takuan, Hakuin 20 Ikkyû's *dôka* 21 Hakuin's Commentary on the Shin-gyô 22 Rennyo's Sayings 23 Zen and the Object of Life 24 Zen and Reality 25 No Japanese Zen, Thank You! 26 Postscript.

9 EDO SATYRICAL VERSE ANTHOLOGIES (Hokuseido, 1961) 1p preface + 331pp + index. General Introduction in 3 sections; 1 History of Oriental Humour 2 European Satire 3 18th Century Edo Satyrical Verse. Other chapter headings as follows; 1 Introduction 2 Mutamagawa, Vols. I-XVII 3 Mankuawase 4 Yanagidaru (including Parodies of the Hyakunin Isshu) 5 Suetsumuhana 6 Kawasoe Yanagi 7 Yanagidaru Shûi 8 Epilogue.

10 A HISTORY OF HAIKU (in 2 vols.) (Hokuseido, 1964) VOLUME ONE - FROM THE BEGINNINGS UP TO ISSA (1964) 2pp preface + 427 pp. Introduction in 5 chapters: 1 Haiku and Zen 2 Animism 3 Nature in Japanese Literature 4 The English View of Nature 5 Haiku in English Literature. Main body of the work in 23 chapters: 1 Renga 2 Sôgi 3 Sôkan, Moritake 4 Teitoku and the Teimon School 5 Sôin

142

and the Danrin School 6 Pre-Bashô Haiku Poets 7 Onitsura 8 Bashô 9 The Ten Disciples of Bashô-I 10 The Ten Disciples of Bashô-II 11 Others of the Bashô School - I 12 Others of the Bashô School - II 13 Women Haiku Writers 14 Haiku between Bashô and Buson 15 Buson-I 16 Buson-II 17 Taigi 18 Poets of Buson's Time-I 19 Poets of Buson's Time-II 20 Issa-I 21 Issa-II 22 Issa-III 23 Issa-IV. VOLUME TWO - FROM ISSA UP TO THE PRESENT (1964) 46pp introduction +363pp + index. Introduction in 6 chapters: 1 Technical Terms 2 Renga 3 Haiku and Chinese Poetry 4 Season Words and Brevity in Haiku 5 Haiga 6 Haiku, the Poetry of Sensation. Main body of the work in 19 chapters: 24 Poets of Issa's Time 25 Shiki: the Critic 26 Shiki: on *Furu-ike-ya* 27 Shiki: the Haiku Poet 28 The Meiji Era 29 Meiji Poets - I 30 Meiji Poets - II 31 Meiji Poets - III 32 Santôka 33 The New Haiku 34 The Shôwa Era - I 35 The Shôwa Era - II 36 Modern Poets - I 37 Modern Poets - II 38 Modern Poets - III 39 Modern Poets - IV 40 The 'Best' Modern Haiku 41 Summary 42 World Haiku.

(Blyth also edited 7 anthologies of literature with general themes, such as 'A Chronological Anthology of Nature in English Literature '(Kairyudo, 1949) and 'A Chronological Anthology of Religion in English Literature '(Bunkyo-shorin, 1951); and 7 editions of English writers for Japanese students (R.L.Stevenson (2), Thoreau (2); Hazlitt, Emerson, Dorothy Wordsworth). In addition, he wrote 5 language teaching books for Japanese students (4 of English, 1 of Korean); and various pamphlets.)

146